PENGUIN PASSNOTES

Gregory's Girl

Susan Quilliam was born in Liverpool
University. After a period of teaching, si.   she
now works as a freelance writer. She has w.   study
guides in the Penguin Passnotes series, inclu   *y Family and
Other Animals* and *A Taste of Honey*.

PENGUIN PASSNOTES

GERALD COLE

Gregory's Girl

based on the film by Bill Forsyth

SUSAN QUILLIAM
ADVISORY EDITOR: STEPHEN COOTE, M.A., Ph.D.

PENGUIN BOOKS

Penguin Books Ltd, 27 Wrights Lane, London W8 5TZ (Publishing and Editorial)
and Harmondsworth, Middlesex, England (Distribution and Warehouse)
Viking Penguin Inc., 40 West 23rd Street, New York, New York 10010, USA
Penguin Books Australia Ltd, Ringwood, Victoria, Australia
Penguin Books Canada Ltd, 2801 John Street, Markham, Ontario, Canada L3R 1B4
Penguin Books (NZ) Ltd, 182–190 Wairau Road, Auckland 10, New Zealand

First published 1988

Copyright © Susan Quilliam, 1988
All rights reserved
Interactive approach developed by Susan Quilliam

Extracts from Roger McGough, *Sky in the Pie*,
reprinted by permission of A. D. Peters & Co. Ltd

Made and printed in Great Britain by
Richard Clay Ltd, Bungay, Suffolk
Filmset in Monophoto Ehrhardt

Except in the United States of America, this book is sold subject
to the condition that it shall not, by way of trade or otherwise, be lent,
re-sold, hired out, or otherwise circulated without the
publisher's prior consent in any form of binding or cover other than
that in which it is published and without a similar condition
including this condition being imposed on the subsequent purchaser

Contents

To the Student

The purpose of this book is to help you appreciate Gerald Cole's novelization of Bill Forsyth's film *Gregory's Girl*. It will help you to understand details of the plot. It will also help you to think about the characters, about what the writer is trying to say and how he says it. These things are most important. After all, understanding and responding to plots, characters and ideas are what make books come alive for us.

You will find this Passnote most useful after you have read *Gregory's Girl* through at least once. A first reading will reveal the plot and make you think about the lives of the people it describes and your feelings for them. Now your job will be to make those first impressions clear. You will need to read the book again and ask yourself some questions. What does the writer really mean? What do I think about this incident or that one? How does the writer make such and such a character come alive?

This Passnote has been designed to help you do this. It offers you background information. It also asks many questions. You may like to write answers to some of these. Others you can answer in your head. The questions are meant to make you think, feel and respond. As you answer them, you will get a clearer knowledge of the book and of your own ideas about it. When your thoughts have become clear, then you will be able to write confidently because you will have made yourself an alert and responsive reader.

Page numbers at section headings and in parentheses refer to the Fontana paperback edition of *Gregory's Girl*.

Introduction

Gordon John Sinclair emerges from the stage door of the West End theatre where he's currently appearing and smiles benevolently down at me from a great height. The film is not deceptive. 'Gregory' is as tall, and as gangling, in real life.

He is also as friendly, as easy-going and as endearing as Gregory seems in the film. 'I've got an hour between shows . . .' he says tentatively, in a strong Scottish accent. 'Shall we go and grab a bite to eat?'

On the way, at a street crossing, two girls rush up to him with whoops of joy and strong American accents: 'Aren't you . . . yes, you are!' I hesitate, expecting the off-duty actor's brush-off routine, but John Gordon Sinclair, as he is known to his fans, is equally eager, happy to chat – 'Did you enjoy the show, then?' – and seemingly genuinely interested in them as people.

Leaving the two thrilled Americans at the next street corner, we head for a restaurant to combine talk and food. The interview proceeds slowly, interrupted by squeals of delight as various members of the restaurant staff spot him and come over for a chat. He is obviously both well-known and popular; but equally obviously he believes what he is saying when he turns to me and admits, 'I'm terribly shy; I'd love acting if only people wouldn't come and watch me.'

He is a delight to interview, unselfconscious, revealing – and very happy to talk about *Gregory's Girl*, despite the fact that the film was made seven years ago.

'I was working as an electrician,' and going to the Glasgow Youth Theatre, an after-work (or after-school) drama group which seems to have been a total inspiration for all involved. Gordon John Sinclair speaks enthusiastically of the classes, the improvisations – and of Bill Forsyth, whose involvement with the Youth Theatre was to prove so crucial.

Forsyth is Gordon's hero, a documentary film maker, who made his first venture into features with *That Sinking Feeling* in which Gordon was also involved. Then, after years of planning, thinking and playing around with ideas, 'Bill disappeared for months, and turned up on my doorstep one evening out of the blue.'

He announced that he'd been away raising the money for the film – and had returned to offer Gordon the part of Gregory. At first, Gordon laughs as he remembers it, the eighteen-year-old apprentice electrician couldn't quite take it in. 'I kept saying: "you'll have to pay me, you know. I can't take time off work just like that."' Forsyth did pay, and Gordon did take the time off work, six of the most hardworking, and happiest, weeks of his life.

'I loved everything about it – apart from the outdoor location shots, when people hung round and stared.'

The film was developed from improvisations at the Glasgow Youth Theatre, but was firmly set in real life, in the sort of Scottish new town where 'there's nothing but screaming kids and young couples', and lads like Gregory grow up slowly and painfully.

How much of Gordon is there in Gregory? He smiles disarmingly. 'I should say a lot. But there's more of Bill [Forsyth] in there than there is of me . . .' He talks at length about the horrors of growing up, the awkward years between childhood and adulthood when 'you discover girls can talk'. Faced by all this, Gregory just becomes 'a looney . . . he's totally mad.'

What about the other characters – Dorothy, Susan, the grown-ups? Dorothy, it appears, is the *'femme fatale* . . . a girl who can play football . . . what more can you want?' One gets the impression of real enthusiasm here, and Gordon certainly rejects any notion that Dorothy is seen, in the film, to be cruel or unfeeling. Whether or not the real-life Gordon is biased (he and Dee Hepburn, the girl who plays Dorothy, went out together during the making of the film), it's not, in his opinion, Dorothy's fault either that Gregory falls for her, or that she doesn't fall for him.

Equally, it is just as natural that Gregory and Susan are 'right for each other.' He talks enthusiastically about their relationship, 'they're on the same wavelength' – and also about his own scenes with Clare Grogan, who plays Susan in the film. Their final scenes together, dancing, and walking together in the twilight, are his favourites. In his opinion, too, Gregory and Susan will stay together, 'and probably get married when they're twenty.'

We talk about the meaning of the film. For Gordon, it is about growing up – and I get the impression that he draws the thinnest of dividing lines between Gregory's growing-up process and his own. He talks of boys coming to terms with their own adulthood, their own sexuality; he speaks of girls who are older, more mature, 'in control'. When asked what single thing he would like to say to young people, his immediate response is a wry 'that it doesn't last for ever'; *it* being adolescence.

And after the film? At first, everyone involved with *Gregory's Girl* assumed it would never be noticed. When it was – when it was acclaimed at the National Film Festival, shown in major cinemas, turned into a book, set for examinations – no one was more surprised than Gordon.

'Bill Forsyth and I went down Sauchiehall Street in Glasgow, to this cinema . . . and just stood there looking at the posters and taking snaps of it all.' And the boy who had gone back to his apprenticeship as an electrician suddenly found himself with a potential career as an actor. He never did any drama training – 'I work on instinct,' and now, at twenty-five, with a string of successful roles behind him, he is ready for a change.

'I want to direct . . . I'm thinking of taking a course in America.' His face lights up as he tells me about a promotion video he made – wrote, directed, designed – himself. 'I remember going into the studio and seeing the set they'd just made, and it was just as I'd designed it; it was my twenty-fifth birthday, and it was the best birthday present I'd ever had . . .'

We leave the restaurant, in a flurry of goodbyes from the staff, to get Gordon back to his theatre in time for his next performance. He is nine years older than the sixteen-year-old Gregory. He is an actor and budding director, not a schoolboy taking his CSEs. He is charming, at ease – a far cry from Gregory's adolescent turmoils.

Why is it then that I have to stop myself, as we say goodbye, from adding –

'Oh, and – good luck, Gregory . . .'

Synopsis of Gregory's Girl

CHAPTER 1

Gregory Underwood is happy. He is sixteen years old, and ready to fall in love.

At the moment, he's playing a game of football, his first love; but his mind isn't really on the game. He is so absent-minded that he gets hit on the head by a flying ball, and is told off by his gym teacher, Phil Menzies.

It's a bit late for reprimands. The team fall behind six-nil. Gregory is struck by the sheer madness of such complete and utter failure.

Back in the changing room after the game, Phil Menzies tells Gregory off again, and threatens to withdraw him from the team. Gregory is shocked by this.

The tension is broken by Phil's cigarette burning down. Phil decides to put Gregory in goal for three weeks on trial, and then to review the situation. Gregory is grateful, though Phil is sure he has been too soft on him.

CHAPTER 2

On his way home, Gregory ponders about what has happened, and realizes that he is not too worried about it. In fact, he is not too worried about anything at the moment – which worries him.

Walking on, he meets an old schoolfriend, Gary, who is now working as a traffic counter. Gregory is envious that Gary seems much more mature than him, and is then overcome by the news that Gary's girlfriend is going to have a baby, and that the two of them are going to get married.

Gregory is particularly jealous of the fact that Gary has slept with a girl. He walks home, determined to 'get a woman'.

That night, Gregory goes off to find his friends, who are hiding outside a nurses' home, waiting to see the nurses undressing.

When he meets Andy, Eric, Pete and Charlie, they are avidly watching one lighted window where a young nurse, all unawares, is taking off first her dress, then her slip, to reveal her bra. The boys are overcome with delight, and leave satisfied.

As they go, two much younger boys emerge from the undergrowth and watch as the nurse goes on to remove her bra . . .

CHAPTER 3

The next morning, Gregory oversleeps and is late for school. He dresses, grabs a bite of breakfast and walks to the bus stop.

On the way, he sees a crowd of toddlers from the estate; he realizes that he'd settle for marriage and a family, with all that involved, just for the 'independence and money and a woman waiting at home every night . . .'

As he gets on the bus, he realizes with delight that it is being driven by his favourite female driver. He is then embarrassed beyond belief when the very nurse he watched undress last night gets on the bus. Gregory gets off at once, a stop before school.

Meanwhile, Gregory's dad, a driving instructor, is amazed to find a loping figure heading down the middle of the road in front of the panicking learner driver. It is Gregory completing his walk to school; he greets his dad happily, then trots off again. His dad is left open-mouthed.

And at Gregory's school, his late arrival is watched by some of the staff, particularly Phil Menzies, who mutters dark things about how Gregory's days in the football team are numbered.

CHAPTER 4

Phil, in fact, has ideas for new blood in the team, and is to spend that morning holding trials for new members. On his way out to the field, he meets Gregory, an embarrassing encounter all round.

Phil greets those boys there for the trial, and sets them off on ball-control exercises. As he does, he notices a girl coming towards him; and the next minute she is informing him that she has come for the trial. After a short argument Phil is forced to give in and let her join the boys.

Gregory is watching. He sees the girl move on to the field – and play exquisite football. 'Magic,' breathes Gregory. His friends recognize that something odd is happening – Gregory is falling in love.

When the trial is over, the girl, Dorothy, challenges Phil Menzies. He is unwilling to include her in the team, but has to admit that she was the best. Gregory is entranced.

CHAPTER 5

Gregory is in love. Dorothy has become the centre of his world.

In cookery, where he is paired with his friend Steve, a master cook, he can think of no one else. Even when pretty Susan comes over to ask Steve's help with her cooking, he is not distracted from thoughts of Dorothy.

He tells Steve, who reacts with supreme unconcern to Gregory's revelations, and tells him he has no chance with Dorothy. For the first time, Gregory becomes a little less than ecstatic.

CHAPTER 6

Andy and Charlie, Gregory's friends, are feeling put out. They know about Gregory's feelings. They see all around them girls and boys enjoying each other's company. They are desperate to join in. Meanwhile Pete is in the girls' playground, asking Dorothy if he can borrow her personal football to practise with. Dorothy refuses point blank, and Pete walks off, leaving the girls discussing whether he is still a virgin. The talk turns to Gregory, and Susan tells Dorothy how keen he is on her. Dorothy is scornful.

Her ardent admirer, in the meantime, has gone into training, desperate to stay in the football team and stay near Dorothy.

But, in the next game, as Dorothy totally dominates the play, he lets a goal in, and lets himself down. Dorothy hardly notices him.

Later, in the changing room, Dorothy asks an embarrassed Gregory if he has any sticking plaster, and he is able to oblige. They chat for a while, about their childhoods, about Italy, Gregory becoming more and more enamoured, until the arrival of Gordon and Eric spoils everything.

Gordon wants to interview Dorothy for the school magazine, and she seems only too willing. Finally, Gregory's patience snaps, and he shoos them out of the changing room, and sulkily gets changed.

CHAPTER 7

Desperate to impress Dorothy, Gregory applies to learn Italian, though the Italian teacher is less than convinced that he is really committed to the subject.

Back in his English lesson, the class is studying *A Midsummer Night's Dream*, but Gregory doesn't concentrate, having noticed that Dorothy is in the room.

The lesson is disturbed by the arrival of the window cleaners, one of whom turns out to be Billy, an ex-pupil of the school. The English teacher greets him like an old friend, and chats to him. Gregory starts to relax.

Phil Menzies, meanwhile, has been called to the Head's office. He waits outside while the Head finishes negotiating with Steve about the food for the Parent–Teacher Association tea. When Phil does get to see the Head, he finds that the issue is Dorothy.

Unsure whether the Head is pleased or displeased at there being a girl in the football team, Phil parries, and is relieved to find that the Headmaster approves. His only worry is whether there will be any 'hanky-panky'. Phil thinks of tough, no-nonsense Dorothy and laughs to himself at the very thought.

CHAPTER 8

After school, Gregory's sister Madeleine waits for him. They get on well, and she is going to help him choose some new clothes – she knows all about Dorothy.

While she waits, Madeleine is offered not only company on the walk home, but also a cigarette from Billy, who is waiting for his old schoolfriend, Steve. She refuses both.

When Gregory appears, with Andy and Steve, the group walk a little way together, and then Gregory and Madeleine walk off to the shopping precinct. Gregory is very aware of how jealous he is of Billy.

When they arrive at the clothes shops, Madeleine seems to know exactly what will suit Gregory, and is able to talk him out of his rather conservative tastes. She also cheers him up by talking about Dorothy. When they stop for a drink, Gregory is seized with a sudden fierce desire to act – to approach Dorothy as soon as possible.

CHAPTER 9

Gregory is talking to Steve, asking him what he meant when he said Gregory had 'no chance' with Dorothy. At first, Steve seems only interested in the cookery programme on the television and, when he does talk to Gregory, is irritatingly practical and dismissive.

The bell goes. It is Madeleine's friend, Richard, wanting to take Madeleine for a walk. Gregory suddenly feels overwhelmingly jealous and appalled, and snaps at Richard, who seems very calm and under-standing.

Later that evening, Gregory sits in his bedroom pining for Dorothy. He has decided to act, and now he wants the opportunity to do so. As he caterwauls back at the tom-cats nearby, three streets away Susan hears the noise and thinks of Gregory. It makes her smile.

In school the next day, Gregory heads for the darkroom, where Eric is developing the photos of Dorothy he took for the school magazine. Gregory buys a print from him for twenty-five pence.

On his way to his form room, his world is shattered when a small girl from the junior year brings him a message from Dorothy. She wants to see him at breaktime. Gregory begins to hope.

CHAPTER 10

At breaktime, Gregory tidies himself in the gents, forcibly borrowing a junior's comb to do so. Then he heads for his rendezvous with Dorothy.

He is a bit perturbed that there are other girls with her, but floats on air when she asks him to spend the lunchtime with her practising football. When he leaves, having happily agreed to the arrangement, Susan follows him with her eyes in a fascinated way.

Gregory is in heaven. He stumbles through the school, smiles happily as he notices Phil Menzies ogling Miss Welch, and heads off to find Steve.

Steve has opened a new outlet for his cakes, in the toilets. As he surveys his empire, Gregory tries to persuade him to lend his new jacket for the date with Dorothy that Gregory is sure will follow the lunchtime practice session. Steve agrees. Gregory's ecstasy is only spoiled by finding the self-same print of Dorothy he bought from Eric for twenty-five pence on sale in the toilets for ten pence.

Andy and Charlie are still talking about girls. They approach Carol and Margo at lunchtime, but totally fail to make anything but a bad impression on the girls.

Gregory is having a hard time with Dorothy, who is running rings round him on the football field. But he keeps going, desperately hanging on to the chance that she might go out with him.

Andy's chat-up tactics fail to work with Susan . . .

CHAPTER 11

The lunchtime football session is nearly over, and Gregory is exhausted. At the end, Dorothy simply walks away.

Gregory is desperate. He runs after her, and, terror in his eyes, asks for a date.

Dorothy agrees, to Gregory's utter amazement. She even agrees after he has queried her agreement – and she arranges to meet him – at half-past seven in the shopping precinct. Gregory is numb with happiness.

Phil Menzies pops his head into the girls' changing room, and finds Dorothy there. They start to chat. Dorothy wants to make peace with Phil; the gym teacher is increasingly impressed with Dorothy's talent and commitment to the game. As she practises a new football movement that he teaches her, he realizes that he is, quite unexpectedly, feeling very happy.

Gregory is preparing for his date, helped by Madeleine, who is maternal, supportive and giggly. Gregory too is feeling very happy.

CHAPTER 12

'He was feeling bad.' It is seven forty-five, and there is no sign of Dorothy. He had begun to have his doubts when he left home, but now he is panicking.

When a figure approaches, he panics even more – and then discovers it is Carol, with the news that Dorothy is not coming. Gregory is desolate, but recovers himself sufficiently to suggest that he and Carol go and buy some chips.

On the way, Carol pops into a telephone box; a few minutes later, she emerges dressed punk-style, to greet a horrified Gregory. He wants to leave then and there, but she pulls him along to the fish and chip shop. Here Carol tells him that Dorothy fancies a student from the college of Physical Education. She leaves him with Margo.

Gregory is by now totally bemused, and will go along with anything. While Margo makes a phone call, he chats to Andy and Charlie. When she emerges, he happily follows her, and even when she rebuffs his tentative pass, goes with her, even though he is beginning to fear the worst.

Susan is waiting, all dressed up. She has just received Margo's phone call, and is feeling very pleased with the way the plan is working.

The next minute, Margo and Gregory appear, and the minute after that, Margo has gone and Gregory is alone with Susan. Then he realizes that the whole thing was a set-up, designed to get him on a date with Susan.

He feels flattered. He takes another look at Susan, and likes what he sees. And when she suggests they go to the country park, he is even more delighted.

They get on well, laughing and talking together. They meet some of Gregory's friends, all of whom are impressed that he is with Susan. Gregory begins to understand the advantages of being with a girl he can talk to – and he also realizes that he has hardly thought about Dorothy.

Walking home, they link arms. At Gregory's doorstep they kiss; easy, enjoyable kisses that make Gregory wonder why he was ever frightened of it all. They arrange to see each other the next day in school, and part happily and hopefully.

Madeleine is waiting up for Gregory. He tells her all about it, and they tease each other. Finally she asks: 'Who's going to be Gregory's girl . . .?' He retorts 'You are!'

Left alone, Gregory thinks with amazement at how he used to want Dorothy – and with equal wonder at how he now wants Susan. Life is good. Gregory Underwood is happy.

Commentary

CHAPTER 1

Section 1, *pp. 5–7*

'Gregory Underwood was happy.' So the book begins, immediately introducing us to the two main issues in the book – the hero and his emotions.

Gregory, we learn, is sixteen. He's growing up. His father, a driving instructor, says that he's grown a good five inches in the last year. It's a difficult time, in body and mind. Changes are happening. Gregory is becoming a new person.

We meet him first on the football field; football, we learn, is his first love. But, at the moment, he's losing interest in football. He's more interested in falling in love.

As if to prove that Gregory's fading interest in football is not all in his imagination, he's hit on the head by a ball he doesn't even see, let alone react to. As a result, he gets a few sharp words from his gym teacher.

Gregory doesn't worry. He just smiles. He quite likes the teacher, Phil Menzies, particularly because he's easy to wind up.

Just at that moment, Gregory's team, Climackton Comprehensive, gets possession – but all too quickly loses it, and suffers another goal. Amidst cheers from the other side, and swearing from his own team, Gregory suddenly sees the funny side of things, and starts laughing. The Climackton side don't appreciate Gregory's laughter at all.

This first section of the first chapter introduces us to the book, the hero and the main issues.

Read through it again, and begin to jot down notes about what you learn of Gregory. How old is he, what sort of person is he? Do you think you'd like him if you met him?

The other two characters mentioned that occur later in the book are Phil Menzies and Andy, Gregory's friend. What impression do you get of them?

Then, think about the issues that the book is dealing with. They're all mentioned in this first section – growing up, love and sex, the school situation.

This section is supposed to draw you into the book, and the film, to make you want to know more, to help you sympathize with, or identify with, the main character. Does it succeed?

Section 2, *pp. 7–11*

Back in the changing room, Gregory begins to get dressed. Just as he's finished, and is putting on his earring, wondering whether to spend the evening in the pub, Phil Menzies arrives.

The teacher is depressed about the game, and Gregory's reaction of philosophical humour doesn't help. Phil gets angry. How could Gregory have reacted that would have calmed Phil down – or do you think the teacher himself should have joined in the laughter?

In the end, Gregory does try to make amends, but only makes things worse by referring to football as 'only a game' (p. 8). Phil attacks Gregory's performance, pointing out that he's a striker and should be scoring goals. Gregory defends himself by pointing out how much he's grown lately, and how off-putting it is.

As Gregory talks to Phil, he suddenly notices that the master is growing a moustache; but Phil is still concerned with football. He tells Gregory that he's thinking of dropping him from the team. Gregory's startled and unintentional defiance creates tension between them, broken only by Phil's cigarette burning down.

He backs away, physically and in every other respect. Gregory too calms down, and says that he's finished growing now and will soon have his old form back. Their uneasy truce results in Phil giving Gregory a trial period of three weeks in goal and, relieved to be let off suspension, Gregory agrees. He leaves quite happily, though Phil is already beginning to regret what he has done.

The relationship between Gregory and Phil Menzies is a theme running through the book. How would you describe it? It shows us a number of things about Phil, and about Gregory and the way his relationship to other people, and to other adults, is changing.

What do you learn from this encounter about Gregory and the way he relates to Phil? Make some notes, then write an account of the argument from Phil's point of view, showing how you felt during it.

CHAPTER 2

Section 1, *pp. 12–16*

Gregory is on his way home. He gets off the bus and heads for the housing estate where he lives.

He feels a bit depressed, mainly because he seems so removed from everything; even the thought of being dropped from the First Eleven seems to leave him unmoved. He thinks about leaving school, going into the 'real world' (p. 12).

His thoughts are interrupted by a splash of soapy water from the team of motorway cleaners hard at work. 'Teamwork' thinks Gregory happily – that's what being grown-up is about (p. 13). He drifts off into a fantasy when, suddenly, he sees a familiar figure.

Gary, an ex-schoolfriend of Gregory's, is on the motorway bridge. He is hard at work counting the traffic, and can hardly spare the time to talk to Gregory. Gregory asks about the work, the money. Gary defends his job vigorously, proud of what he's doing.

Then he drops a bombshell. He and his girlfriend are getting married, and are going to have a baby. Gregory is shattered, particularly when he learns that Gary and Fiona slept together during a party Gregory himself was at.

Embarrassed, Gregory makes his exit, while Gary, lost in his world of traffic counting, hardly sees him go.

Alone, Gregory realizes how stunned he is. Gary seems far superior to him, with a job, marriage, a baby on the way. Particularly, Gregory envies Gary his sexual experience. He himself got no more than a peck of a kiss from that party. He realizes that it is now or never. He has to get a woman.

This section brings Gregory out of the school situation and face-to-face with the real world. Other people of his age are working and starting families. He envies them.

Do you think he should? How adult is Gary, and how successful do you think he will be in his future? What do you think of him as a person – is he responsible, and is he mature? How grown-up is he?

Gregory sees Gary's situation from the outside and envies it. What do you think Gary feels about Gregory? How do you feel about your friends who have stopped studying and gone out to work – and how do they feel about you?

Gregory's main envy is of Gary's sexual experience. Have you ever felt like this? Do you think Gary ever did?

Section 2, *pp. 16–21*

That evening, Gregory goes out in search of his friends. He has already called at Andy's house, and at Eric's, but both were out. He has checked the pub and the country park. They can only be at the nurses' home, so Gregory goes there.

He climbs the side of a grassy hill, making silly faces and silly noises – and getting a very odd stare from a passing nurse. Gregory tries to pretend he's got cramp.

Over the fence, Gregory is in the grounds of the nurses' home. He pretends to be Clint Eastwood, prepared for violent action – and almost immediately hears his friends' voices, and startles them in the undergrowth. Eric, Andy, Charlie and Pete are there, and the group of boys settles down to watch.

They are concentrating on a lighted window in the nurses' home, where a young girl dressed in a slip is taking off a nurse's cap. The boys are agog at the sight of a girl wearing so little. When she goes back inside the room and reappears wearing only a bra, they are deliriously happy. Andy begins to count the seconds they can see her, and makes such a fuss that they have to drag him back into the undergrowth in case they're seen.

The boys are all ecstatic, and when the nurse disappears from view, are content to leave. As they go, two much younger boys emerge from the undergrowth. They are obviously quite used to seeing nurses in their underwear, and are scornful of the older lads' ecstasy. As they watch, the nurse takes her bra off.

This section gives yet another view of Gregory's developing attitude to sex. In the last section, we saw sex leading to babies and marriage. Here, it is pure lust.

But it's an innocent lust. The younger boys wait to see the nurse undress completely, while Gregory and his friends think the night is complete with only a glimpse of a bra.

How would you describe Gregory's attitude to sex – choose as many of these phrases as you think are appropriate, and then write a paragraph on 'Gregory and sex'.

1. Gregory is sexually experienced.
2. Gregory is quite ready to sleep with a girl.
3. Gregory has no idea what sex is about.
4. Gregory feels attracted by and scared of sex.
5. Gregory thinks women are wonderful.
6. Gregory actually is quite innocent about sex.

Do you think Gregory is morally wrong to be watching the girl? What do you think he would say if you told him he was wrong? How do you think the girl would react if she knew she had been watched?

The scene is also quite funny in places. If you've seen the film, you'll know where the laughter should come. If you haven't, try to work that out. What is funny about the whole scene – and are we meant to laugh at Gregory and his friends?

CHAPTER 3

Section 1, *pp. 22–7*

The following morning, Gregory wakes late. He's been dreaming of the dark-haired nurse playing football beside him, neatly combining his two loves in one. (How does this dream actually come true later in the book?)

He becomes aware that the house is quiet, and realizes with a start that his father has gone to work and his mother has taken his sister Madeleine to the dentist. He has overslept.

He leaps out of bed, and carefully closes the curtains before dressing. (Why is this ironic?) In the bathroom, he rumples his hair and pouts at the mirror, trying to look like a rock star. He raids the kitchen for things to eat, though he doesn't steal his sister's favourite chocolate bar. Then, earring in place, he sets off for school.

On his way to the bus stop, Gregory meets a horde of toddlers, and, maybe remembering Gary, stops to think that he quite likes them.

They don't have to worry about impressing girls, unlike him. It seems unfair that at his age neither adults nor girls of his own age regard him as grown-up. He tries to cheer himself up by pretending he's a football star, but then remembers his spots and blushes, and calms down again.

He thinks of Gary and Fiona again. He realizes that he wouldn't mind being in their situation. At least he would be his own person, with his own money, and would have a woman to come home to.

The bus comes along, just as he is bemoaning his fate.

In this section, for the first time, we see Gregory at home. We see him getting up in the morning, and going to school.

You should by now have a fairly full picture of what Gregory is like, and be starting to form an impression of him as a person. Is he likeable? Does the author (and the director of the film) mean us to like him? Make two lists: one of things you like about Gregory, one of things you think are stupid or silly. If you can, compare your list with a friend and see if you agree.

One person mentioned in this section who will be important later on is Gregory's sister, Madeleine. We know from just the one brief reference what sort of relationship he has with her. What is it like?

Gregory is still worried about sex. It seems as if, at the moment, exams, football and girls are of equal importance in his life, and he doesn't quite know which one to worry about. But sex is gradually becoming more and more important to him. Why do you think the scene with the toddlers is included? What is it meant to show us?

Section 2, *pp. 27–9*

When Gregory gets on the bus, he is delighted to find that his favourite woman driver is on board. He sees her as a romantic vision of loveliness, and can think of nothing else as he bumps into people in his eagerness to get to her.

In his eagerness, he also gives her the wrong bus fare, and then is mortified with shame when she points this out. He blushes, feeling himself ridiculous, and then catches her smile. Instantly, he transforms it into a smile between equals, sure that she is flashing him a subtle sexual signal. For a moment, he sees himself as a man of the world.

Then, the bus stops at the Nurses' Annex and, to Gregory's horror, one of the nurses who boards the bus is the one whom he and his friends had spied on the previous night. He is hideously embarrassed. At his stare, the nurse lowers her head, and he realizes that she is only a little older than he is – and feels even more embarrassed, and excited.

He gets off the bus a stop early, and walks the rest of the way to school, in order to escape.

In this section, we learn more of Gregory's attitude to girls. First, the bus driver, a distant figure totally out of Gregory's reach. He worships her from afar, and imagines she is flashing him subtle signals. What do you think she is actually thinking, and feeling; look particularly at how she addresses him.

Second, the nurse, who embarrasses Gregory. Suddenly, he sees her as a real person, and not just as a sexual object. He gets confused, and aroused. What is the nurse feeling as she notices him watching her? Choose some of these words and include them in a paragraph written as if you were the nurse, having just seen Gregory on the bus.

flattered	uneasy
embarrassed	excited
alarmed	frightened
pleased	curious
concerned	surprised
shy	uncertain

Have you ever worshipped someone from afar? Have you ever noticed someone watching you, and realized they fancy you? How have you reacted? And how would you have liked to have reacted?

Section 3, *pp. 29–33*

Meanwhile, Gregory's dad is teaching a driving lesson. He worries, as he often does, that his pupil might be a maniac. His pupil, Mr Clark, is a strange man, a redundant rent clerk who seems very unsure of how to drive. Mr Underwood worries even more.

This is very unlike him, as he is normally a placid man. But he is being made nervous by his children – Madeleine's 'normality' and Gregory's odd behaviour. Gregory apparently came home last night covered in leaf-mould. (What was he doing?) Mr Underwood isn't frantic with concern, because he knows Gregory is too idealistic to be a criminal but, even so, he worries.

As the car moves on, Mr Underwood suddenly sees a pedestrian, running along in the middle of the road. He is hypnotized. Neither the pedestrian nor Mr Clark seem to have noticed anything different happening, while Mr Underwood is quietly panicking.

The pedestrian slaps the car bonnet, and Mr Underwood slams the brakes on. He recognizes Gregory and calls out to him, while Mr Clark complains about the unscheduled emergency stop.

Mr Underwood and Gregory greet each other. Mr Underwood is determinedly and kindly sarcastic, Gregory seems anxious to get away.

Finally, his dad, in a desperate attempt to get communication, comments on the fact that he never sees Gregory, and asks him to be around for breakfast on Friday. Gregory has to agree, then runs off. Mr Underwood, feeling rather pleased with the outcome of the conversation, drives on.

We only meet Gregory's dad once in the book, and his mum only by reference. What sort of a person does Mr Underwood seem? Notice the gentle, but sarcastic, way he treats Gregory, which Gregory doesn't seem to notice.

Why do you think this scene is included in the book at this point? Choose as many of these reasons as you think are correct, and then expand them to a paragraph, explaining why the scene is there. Refer to the rest of the book if you want to.

1. To show us Gregory's character.
2. To show us his dad's character.
3. To show us Mr Clark's character.
4. To show us how Gregory could be when he grows up.
5. To include some more humour.
6. To give us some insight into driving instructors.
7. To provide some excitement in the book.
8. To show us the relationship between Gregory and his dad.

What is funny about this scene? Write down as many things as you can think of that are funny. How many of them are similar to things that have happened to you?

Section 4, *pp. 33–6*

At Gregory's school, some of the staff have a free period and are in the staffroom. Alec Wilson, the senior biology master, is staring out of the window, watching Gregory try to sneak in. Alistair Stewart, who teaches religion, joins him in commenting on Gregory scornfully.

When Phil Menzies comes in, he at first thinks they're insulting him, then realizes they're talking about Gregory. But the two masters continue to insult the football team, which annoys Phil just as much. He mutters that he is determined to change the team. Gregory is out, and that very morning he is holding trials for a new striker.

The teachers sip tea and eat cake, made by two of the third-year girls. Phil teases Alec about his friendships with the girls, and Alistair retorts with a comment about Phil's moustache. Embarrassed, he burbles his way out of the room to see to the striker trials.

This section gives us more insight into the teachers. What do you think of them? Notice the way they tease each other, just as Gregory and his friends tease each other. Notice, too, that they seem just as uneasy with the thought of girls as Gregory does. The teasing of Alec is about the fact that some of the younger girls have a crush on him; and the inference is that he encourages this.

What do you learn about education from this scene? Does it remind you of your school or college, or are there any differences?

What do you think this scene is meant to show at this place in the book?

At the end of chapter 3, just before we meet the girl who is to dominate Gregory's thoughts for almost the whole of the rest of the book, what have we learned? How has the author set the scene, by telling us about Gregory, by showing us his family, his school, and the things he is interested in? What issues have been discussed to set the scene for Gregory's passion? What else could the author have told us about Gregory and about the key issues in the book – or do you think he has told us just enough to whet our interest in what will happen next?

CHAPTER 4

Section 1, *pp. 37–43*

Phil Menzies sets off for the striker trials. He's torn between thinking that football is the answer to everything for the school, and that success is only just round the corner; and that something dreadful is going to happen. Then he sees Gregory.

Phil mistrusts Gregory; he doesn't take football seriously enough. So when he realizes that he can't avoid facing him, Phil simply grunts at Gregory that he may have news for him later.

Gregory is bemused. He has just missed the start of the second lesson, and has drifted off into a daydream where he is rescuing his bus driver from terrorists. Now he doesn't know what to do, or where to go. He follows Phil to the playing field.

Phil is pleased that nearly a dozen lads have turned up for the trials, though their energy – and their apparel – leave much to be desired. He starts to lecture to the boys on what a good striker does, and when one of the youngsters queries him, simply dismisses him for not having the right shoes. He starts the boys off with simple ball control, and sends them off down the field, shouting after them.

Just then, Phil becomes aware of a girl approaching from the school. He recognizes her as Dorothy, one of the beauties of the fifth form, whom he normally avoids because they are so tempting, and out of bounds. When he asks her what she wants, the girl replies, 'I'm here for the trial' (p. 41).

At first Phil doesn't understand. When he realizes that Dorothy wants to try for a place in the team, he is at first amazed, then thinks she's playing a trick on him, then tries to talk her round. Dorothy is firm: equal opportunities dictate that she must be allowed a trial. As Phil begins to argue, she just takes a ball and defies him. He has to give in, and Dorothy joins the boys, obviously the best from the start. Phil's heart begins to sink.

In this section, enter Dorothy, who for a while combines the two things Gregory loves most – football and sex appeal. But Gregory has not noticed her yet; it is Phil Menzies who has to cope with the fact that Dorothy plays football and is good at it.

Notice, first, how the scene is set up, the way we see what Phil is thinking from the time he leaves the staffroom, until he gives in to Dorothy. Read the passage through again and then arrange these sentences to give an account of his changing feelings.

Phil feels slightly determined.

He realizes he has lost the battle.

He tries to be conciliatory.

He fantasizes about a good future.

He congratulates himself at having avoided an awkward situation.

He decides not to be angry.

He decides to brazen it out.

He takes control of the situation.

He urges people on.

He is confused about what is happening.

Now turn your attention to Dorothy. What do we know about her? What do you think of her? Phil is obviously very wary of her; why do you think this is, and what is meant by the term 'gaol-bait 5 A' (p. 41)?

What do you think Dorothy is thinking as she goes for the trial? Look at the way she reacts to Phil and how she handles him so well, getting exactly what she wants. Write an account of the incident as if you were Dorothy, telling her friends about what happened.

Here is the clearest example yet of the differences between boys and girls, and the prejudice girls can meet; yet Dorothy in fact is a far better player than any of the boys. What do you think this scene is meant to show about boys as compared to girls?

Section 2, *pp. 43–6*

Gregory has followed Phil to the playing field, and is now watching the game. At first he doesn't notice Dorothy but, as Phil gets more wound up, so Gregory's interest is aroused.

But it is not until Dorothy begins to play football that Gregory begins to understand that his world will never be the same. He feels strange 'rather like flu' (p. 44), and focuses in on Dorothy, unable to take his eyes off her. Andy and Charlie, watching his suddenly glazed expression, stand beside him telling him about her, but Gregory hardly hears them, as Dorothy shoots three consecutive goals past Phil Menzies.

And then the trial is over, and the group come back into school.

Gregory feels even stranger and more affected as Dorothy passes him.
She stops beside Phil Menzies and demands to know how she has
done. Phil won't be pinned down, but Dorothy challenges him, and
he has to admit that she is the best and that he may have her in the
team. Gregory is even more impressed, and realizes suddenly, amaz-
ingly, that he has fallen in love . . .

Now Gregory sees Dorothy. It is not particularly her looks that
impress him at first – that comes later. It is her talent at football that
draws him to her.

It is love at first sight Gregory knows nothing at all about Dorothy;
he has no hope of a returned admiration, and so no hope yet of a
steady relationship. He is only interested in worshipping her.

Has this ever happened to you – love at first sight? What attracted
you to the person you liked? Was it their looks, their personality, or
the fact that they were good at some sport or some shared interest?

Do you think Dorothy notices Gregory? What is she far more
interested in? And, again, look at how she confronts and defeats Phil
Menzies' prejudice. She is actually far more effective a personality
than Phil, even though he is much older.

CHAPTER 5

Section 1, *pp. 47–53*

Gregory's life has changed. Dorothy is now the centre of his world.
He writes her name on his schoolbooks, dreams about her constantly.
He decides he has to tell someone, immediately.

Domestic Science gives him the opportunity. Gregory's friend and
cookery partner, Steve, already, at seventeen, a master chef, is in
charge. Gregory obediently shows that his hands are clean and, under
Steve's expert eye, begins to mix a sponge cake. He will tell Steve
when the meal is under way.

They are interrupted by Susan, another girl in the cookery class, who asks Steve's advice on how to make pastry. Steve is sarcastic about her lack of skill – but the floury imprint of his hand on her skirt makes it obvious that he appreciates other aspects of Susan. Gregory, however, only has thoughts for Dorothy, although he 'instinctively' (p. 49) doesn't want to upset Susan.

The talk already on girls, Gregory decides it is time to mention his situation. He casually advises Steve that he ought to try being in love. Steve doesn't take the hint to ask Gregory about his love life, but instead starts to dream about his future, 'expensive' affairs (p. 50).

Eventually, Gregory has to be more direct. He tells Steve about Dorothy, and again gets scant sympathy. Steve knows all about Dorothy, and is rather scathing of her football skill. He is also scathing about the possibility of Gregory's getting anywhere with Dorothy. 'No chance . . . no chance' (p. 52).

Gregory needs to tell someone about his feelings for Dorothy, and chooses Steve, his friend. Just as Dorothy is excellent at a sport normally regarded as a male preserve, so Steve is good at a 'woman's' skill. In fact, he mocks Dorothy, saying that cookery is much more important than football, a neat twist on the normal male outlook – and on the fact that what attracts many men to women is their home-making skills.

What sort of person is Steve? Read through the passage again and make notes on his character, on the way he handles Susan, and the way he reacts to Gregory. What do you think of Steve as a person – do you like him?

What are his ideas on women, on sex, on romance – do you agree with them?

Gregory gets little sympathy from Steve. What more do we learn about Gregory now that his relationship is developing?

In this scene we meet Susan, who is to be important later in the book. What evidence, if any, do you see now of the relationship she and Gregory will have later? Do you learn anything about Susan, her personality, the sort of person she is?

Finally, look at the setting of the scene, in the domestic science class. Do you agree that everyone's education should include cooking, as Gregory's does? What else do you think everyone should learn to have a 'complete' education?

CHAPTER 6

Section 1, *p. 53*

Andy and Charlie, two of Gregory's friends, are sitting in the senior common room, watching two fifth-formers kissing heavily. The lads are depressed because they have no girls; even Gregory has someone to sigh over, even if he never gets anywhere with Dorothy.

This short section continues to set the scene of young people worrying and wondering about sex. While Gregory is pining for Dorothy, Andy is desperate to get a girl, any girl, in any way he can.

Section 2, *pp. 54–6*

Meanwhile Pete, one of the football team, is venturing into the girls' playground to find Dorothy. When he does track her down, she is with her friends, Margo, Liz, Carol and Susan. They are passing a ball easily between them; though when they kick it to Pete, he catches it awkwardly.

Pete asks Dorothy if he can borrow her ball. She refuses point-blank, which totally floors Pete, who apologizes and backs away.

Watching him go, the girls coolly discuss whether Pete is still a virgin. Can you tell by the way a boy walks? If so, Gregory must be a virgin still, for he lopes along just like Pete does. The talk turns to Gregory. Dorothy doesn't rate him, because his football skill is minimal. But does she fancy him? She thinks he is 'a wally' (p. 56).

Susan, however, smiles when she thinks of Gregory, even when she tells Dorothy how much Gregory fancies her. Susan admires Dorothy's glamour.

Carol has the last word by saying that she knows Pete is, in fact, not a virgin.

For the first time, we hear the girls talking together. They are like royalty, in their own corner of the playground, far more skilful and sophisticated than the boys. Pete is totally overawed.

Write about the girls as you see them. Are they like girls you know? Are they likeable? And do you think that, inside, they are as self-confident and sophisticated as they seem?

Notice how Susan's liking for Gregory is being revealed slowly, against a background of talk about sex. Do you notice any differences between the way the girls talk about sex, and the way the boys do? Which do you think is the more grown-up approach?

Section 3, *pp. 56–7*

Gregory goes into training. To the outside world, he is in training for football; he tells Phil Menzies of his plan, and enthusiastically agrees to adopt the rigorous exercise plan Phil suggests for him.

But, secretly, Gregory is in training for love. He dreams of being with Dorothy on the football pitch, playing as striker and goalie, side by side.

In fact, Gregory hasn't really got back his enthusiasm for football; he is motivated by Dorothy alone, and the fact that she plays football is an added bonus.

His interaction with Phil Menzies shows us again the way the two relate to each other, Phil a little unsure and on the defensive, Gregory at ease and enthusiastic.

Have you ever become enthusiastic about anything because someone you fancied was enthusiastic about it?

Section 4, *pp. 57–60*

Later, as Climackton Comprehensive play St Mungo's, the team still seems to be in the wars. Pete loses a header when it hits a spot on his forehead, and Gregory is exhausted from early morning jogging.

Andy, watching the match, reckons it is stupid to have brought a girl into the team. Though Gregory defends her, Andy just thinks Dorothy looks stupid; girls aren't tough enough for football, and they aren't the right shape.

Their argument is interrupted by a beautiful goal from Dorothy which instantly changes Andy's mind for him. He is now all for women in the team, particularly the glamorous Dorothy. The players for Climackton and St Mungo's obviously agree as Dorothy is swamped by a tide of hugs and kisses.

All too soon, though, the game resumes, and the pressure is on Gregory to keep goal. As the St Mungo's players head towards him, he fails to catch the ball and it lands in the net. Humiliated, he retrieves it and gives it back – to an impatient Dorothy.

This is the first time we see Gregory and Dorothy playing together. He is totally outclassed, and knows it – but because he fancies her, and also because he is fair, he defends Dorothy to Andy. Andy himself is eventually won round by sheer performance.

Contrast this game with the other time we've seen Gregory playing, in chapter 1 (pp. 5–7). How does he behave differently? What is the same about him? How has Dorothy's joining the team changed things?

Watch out here, too, for little touches of humour – like all the boys taking advantage of Dorothy's goal to leap on her in a tide of affection.

How does Dorothy handle all this? How do you think she feels? What more do we learn about her from this scene?

Section 5, *pp. 60–7*

After the game, Gregory feels a bit down. He wonders how Dorothy feels about him, and about his botched save. He wonders if in fact Steve is right, that he has no chance with Dorothy. But then again, he loves her. Surely she will respond to that?

The next minute, Dorothy walks into the changing room, asking if Gregory has a plaster. He is totally embarrassed, makes a dive for his tee-shirt, and to his relief finds a plaster in his hold-all.

Dorothy was kicked, but she got her revenge by attacking the boy concerned. This worries Gregory a little, but he ignores it. Dorothy, meanwhile, is reminiscing about other cuts and grazes she's received in her life. She and Gregory exchange stories of childhood injuries, and they laugh together as if they are really close.

However, Gregory is deflated when Dorothy tells him of an Italian boy she knew; he begins to make uncomfortable pictures of Dorothy with another man. He feels excluded when she says she speaks Italian. But with a smile the situation is eased, and Gregory is beginning to relax when the door of the changing room opens and two lads burst in.

Gordon, the editor of the school magazine, and his photographer, Eric, have come to interview Dorothy. Gregory's defensiveness doesn't work; Dorothy is obviously keen to be interviewed, and Gordon moves in enthusiastically. Gregory is forced to take a back seat.

Dorothy fields Gordon's questions expertly, when he asks about the boys' reactions to her being in the team, and about her free time. When he asks her out, she agrees, wanting to please.

Gregory is appalled; he feels threatened and loses his temper. The three leave, Gordon still chatting Dorothy up. Gregory is left feeling disillusioned, angry with Dorothy's Italian friend, angry with Gordon, even angry with Dorothy.

For the first time, Dorothy and Gregory get a chance to talk. It seems as if they could be friends – or could they? Had Gordon and Eric not burst in, what do you think would have happened? Choose one of these options and write about why you think it would have been like that.

1. Gregory would have asked Dorothy out and been rejected.
2. Gregory would have asked Dorothy out and been accepted.
3. Gregory and Dorothy would have chatted for a while, and then Gregory would have left.
4. Dorothy would have got bored and left.
5. Dorothy would have asked Gregory out.
6. Gregory would have tried to kiss Dorothy.
7. Gregory would have become bored with Dorothy.

What do you learn about both of them through their conversation together? In particular, what do you learn about Dorothy by the way she reacts to Gregory?

When Gordon and Eric come in, things change very quickly. Gregory tries to stop them, but is powerless to do so. Why?

Gordon is a very different character to Gregory. How would you describe him? Do you like him? What about the way Dorothy reacts to him – what do you think is running through her mind when she agrees to go out with him?

Finally, what sort of article do you think Gordon will write for the school magazine? Write the article, using everything you think he would have included.

CHAPTER 7

Section 1, *pp. 68–71*

Gregory wants to learn Italian. The Italian teacher, Miss Ford, is suspicious of his motives, and suspects that his interest is in the girls in the class rather than the language.

But Gregory tries hard to convince her of his genuine interest. He spins a tale about wanting to go to Italy to work when he leaves school, and about having some Italian friends. Miss Ford is even less convinced, and suggests Gregory learns technical Italian, which doesn't appeal to him at all. Eventually, she says she'll let him know.

Meanwhile, Phil Menzies has been called in to see the Headmaster. He has no idea why, and the fact worries him. Is he to be congratulated for the football team's draw against St Mungo's? Or perhaps reprimanded for using school funds to buy expensive boots for himself?

As he wonders, Phil meets Gregory, wandering down the corridor declaiming the phrase the Italian teacher has taught him. Scared to meet Gregory, Phil backs into a classroom to avoid him.

Gregory's disillusionment with Dorothy has not lasted long. Now he is trying to get into her Italian class. The teacher has a pretty good idea of what he is doing, and challenges him, but Gregory has no thought that he is being teased. What do you learn about him from this – and the fact that he wants to join the Italian class? Do you think he is wrong to lie about his reasons – and do you think he sees himself as doing wrong?

Think too about what we see of the teachers in this section. Do you think Miss Ford and Phil Menzies are good teachers; and what do you think of them as people?

Section 2, *pp. 71–4*

Back in the English class, Gregory settles down to a lesson about *A Midsummer Night's Dream*, woodenly read aloud by Andy.

Gregory is aware, suddenly, that Dorothy is in the class. He is mesmerized, as usual.

But his attention is taken by a noise at the window. Two window cleaners appear, and one is Billy, an ex-pupil of the school. The English teacher, Miss Welch, is delighted to see the boy, and turns her attention to him. After some interruption from Andy, who is still reading from the play, they chat happily, and Billy cleans Miss Welch's glasses for her.

As he carries on cleaning the windows, Billy mouths at Steve, his former friend in the class, that he will meet him outside at four o'clock.

Another way of looking at school life is shown in this section: an English lesson – and the return of an ex-pupil. How does Miss Welch react to Billy? Say whether you think each of these comments is a fair judgement of the situation.

Miss Welch:

1. Is pleased to see Billy.
2. Is happy to share a joke with him.
3. Is wary of being too familiar with him.
4. Loses control of the class by turning her attention elsewhere.
5. Loses Billy's respect.
6. Feels she has to be polite.
7. Is confident enough to chat with Billy during a class.

Gregory himself will soon be an ex-pupil. How do you think his relationship with the teachers will change when he leaves?

Do you know anyone (maybe yourself) who has left school and then gone back and met the teachers? How did you get on with them? Did you find your relationship with them changed after you left?

Section 3, *pp. 74–5*

In the Headmaster's office, Steve is discussing the arrangements for the forthcoming Parent–Teacher Association tea. The two of them have a neat arrangement going: Steve cooks superbly, the Headmaster pays up. They negotiate like businessmen over price and quality.

The scene shows yet another angle on school life. Steve, only a schoolboy, is the Headmaster's equal here – and relates to him like one. He enjoys negotiating. What does this show you about Steve – and about the Headmaster?

What does it show you about the school?

Section 4, *pp. 75–7*

Phil Menzies is waiting outside the Headmaster's office. He still does not know why he has been called in. The Head's door opens and the Head snaps an order at a boy who is leaving; Phil assumes it is a troublemaker who has just been reprimanded.

Once inside the Head's office, Phil is immediately on the defensive, apologizing for being early. The Head comes to the point: 'There's a girl in the football team' (p. 76).

Phil has no idea how to react, which way the Head is going to jump. He hesitates until he sees that the Head approves, and then with a sigh of relief admits Dorothy's existence.

It is the issue of 'hanky-panky' (p. 77) that the Head is worried about – it takes Phil a long time to realize this. When he does, he is amused; Dorothy herself wouldn't allow anything like that.

*

In this scene, we see Phil Menzies with the Head. Compare the way Phil handles him with the way Steve does. Make two lists; one of the ways Steve reacts to the Headmaster, the other of the ways Phil does. Who is more effective, more grown-up – the teacher or the school-boy?

The other point made here is about sex: the Head is worried that there will be 'hanky-panky' if there's a girl in the team (p. 77). In fact Dorothy isn't in the least interested in that, and would have the strength to stop it if anyone tried anything on. What does this tell you about Dorothy?

CHAPTER 8

Section 1, *pp. 78–81*

Later that afternoon, when the infant and junior school opposite Climackton Comprehensive opens its doors, Gregory notices his sister Madeleine waiting for him.

Gregory gets on well with his sister, better than with any other female he knows. She was the first girl he told about Dorothy. Madeleine, sitting waiting for Gregory, is approached by a boy who likes her; he offers to walk her home. She politely refuses him; she is going shopping with Gregory instead, to buy him new clothes with which to impress Dorothy.

As she sits there, Billy arrives to wait for Steve. He offers Madeleine a cigarette, which she refuses, and chats to her about who she is waiting for. He asks her whether she's 'Gregory's girl' (p. 79). She replies, 'I'm Madeleine.'

When Gregory arrives, with Steve, Charlie and Andy, Billy poses in his smart clothes, smoking his cigarette. Gregory refuses one, partly because he's in training, partly because he wants to set Madeleine a good example.

Billy jokes about Miss Welch, that she fancies him; and this leads on to talk of the nurse they saw through the window the previous week. Embarrassed and uneasy, Gregory turns off with Madeleine to go to the shopping precinct.

We now meet Madeleine, the one girl in Gregory's life whom he really gets on well with. What do you know about her – and about the impression she gives to other people? Make notes about Madeleine under these headings:

What Gregory thinks about her.
What her father thinks about her.
What Richard thinks about her.
What Billy thinks about her.
What you think about her.

Gregory protects her, and wants her to think well of him – how do we know this?

We learn a bit more about Billy, too, as we see him lording it over his ex-classmates. What sort of person is he, and what are we meant to feel about him?

Section 2, *pp. 81–4*

As he and Madeleine walk to the precinct, Gregory feels uneasy at the gap between Billy, in the real world, and himself at school. His life was easy at school, until he met someone like Gary or Billy and was reminded of what life outside was like.

Madeleine begins to realize that Gregory is not, as she thought, dreaming happily of Dorothy, but is in fact getting depressed. So she starts talking about the sort of clothes he ought to buy, and then about Dorothy herself, which cheers Gregory up.

Madeleine says she will give Gregory advice on how to handle Dorothy – in return for the fact that when they were younger he was good to her when other boys were being horrible to their sisters. She tells him to talk to Dorothy, and also to be interested in himself, otherwise he can't expect other people to be interested in him.

Then she drags him off to a café for a drink, and suddenly becomes a little girl again, slurping her ice-cream sundae. Gregory is left with his decision to act now, rather than just keep thinking about Dorothy.

We get to know more about Madeleine here, and like her more and more. Gregory and she obviously get on very well together; how can you tell?

What do you think of Madeleine's advice to Gregory on how to approach Dorothy? Do you agree with her? Is it good advice on romance, on sex? If you were giving Gregory advice, what would you say to him?

In some ways, though Madeleine is much younger than Gregory, she seems to be more mature than he is. Make a list of the ways in which she is more grown-up than Gregory.

CHAPTER 9

Section 1, *pp. 85–8*

Gregory is tackling Steve about his comment that Gregory has 'no chance' (p. 52) with Dorothy. Steve, though, is much more interested in the cookery programme on the television, and eventually Gregory loses his temper, calling Steve a freak for being so obsessive about food.

Steve is bewildered and defensive; hasn't he cooked for Gregory, showing him friendship in the best way he knows? Gregory needs more; he needs sympathy in his crisis. Steve is off-hand and sarcastic, saying that Gregory's problems are unimportant. Anyway, has Gregory actually asked Dorothy for a date?

This gives Gregory the lead-in he needs to ask Steve a favour – will he lend Gregory his white jacket if he does get a date? Steve flatly refuses. At that moment the doorbell rings.

It isn't, as Gregory fantasizes, Dorothy. It is Richard, coming to see if Madeleine is in. Gregory suddenly loses his temper at the thought of someone chatting his sister up, and bawls at the little boy that he's too precocious.

Richard stays calm, offers to shake hands with Gregory, and asks him if he's feeling all right. He has heard about Gregory's passion, from Madeleine. Still enraged, Gregory sends him away.

Here, we see two views of young love. Steve is blasé about it all; food is much more important to him. Notice how his words are reminiscent of what stereotyped 'wives' say to husbands: I cook for you; of course I love you (p. 86).

For Richard, love is spending time with Madeleine because he likes her. He doesn't feel sexual attraction yet. But in some ways, he acts far more maturely than Gregory, who bawls and rages like a father scared for his daughter's virtue.

Make notes on all three characters, and particularly their attitudes to love. Whom do you sympathize with most?

Section 2, *pp. 88–9*

That evening, Gregory is still dressed and awake when everyone else is in bed. He plays with a space toy, thinks about Dorothy, and makes up his mind to act soon. Finally, he leans out of the window and howls with the tom-cats.

A few streets away, Susan also hears the tom-cats, and thinks of Gregory. She rather likes the thought.

Gregory is changing. Part of him is still young, playing with his space toys; but part of him is ready to approach Dorothy, ready to chance rejection to get to know the girl he has worshipped from afar.

Susan is obviously thinking fondly of Gregory. What does 'the girl with a fondness for ostriches' (p. 89) mean?

Section 3, *pp. 89–92*

In school, Gregory visits Eric, who took the pictures of Dorothy for the school magazine. Eric is developing the pictures, and Gregory is entranced.

Eric criticizes Dorothy's shape, but Gregory defends her, as he has in the past, by saying she is 'modern'.

As the pictures develop, Eric annoys Gregory by reminding him how Gordon got a date with Dorothy. Rather than hear the whole story, Gregory asks Eric to give him a print of Dorothy's picture, and after a few minutes haggling, they agree on a price.

As Gregory leaves the darkroom, a small junior girl comes up to him, with a message from Dorothy. She wants to meet Gregory at breaktime in room nine. Gregory is totally shocked. He doesn't know what to think, or whether to hope. All he can do is wait.

After getting a picture of Dorothy from Eric, and being reminded that someone else got a date with her, Gregory is now faced with the fact that Dorothy herself wants to see him. Notice the building up of tension, Gregory's and ours, because we don't know what is going to happen. Unless we have read the book, we don't yet know of Susan's plan – so we don't know whether Gregory will ever get together with Dorothy.

In this section, too, we see more of Eric than before. Like Steve he is already an entrepreneur, and making a profit. Gregory is not at that stage yet. Make notes on what you learn about Eric, and about Gregory, from this section.

In particular, think about what they each think about girls. Eric likes girls to look like girls; Gregory sees Dorothy's 'modernness' as perfect. What do you think?

CHAPTER 10

Section 1, *pp. 93–5*

At break, Gregory doesn't want to rush to room nine in case Dorothy thinks him too eager. Instead, he slips into the toilets and checks his appearance, brushing some hair over a spot. He wishes he had a comb, and notices a first-former combing his hair. When asked, the junior refuses to lend his comb, so Gregory takes it from him by force.

Then he makes his way to room nine. Dorothy is, quite unexpectedly, with a group of other girls. When he greets her, she asks what he's doing at lunchtime, and suggests they practise football together. Gregory is enthralled, certain that the relationship is developing in just the way he wants.

As he leaves, the girls seem bored by him. All except Susan, who seems mesmerized. Dorothy moves to the window to look over the crowded boys' playground, and the girls exchange mocking comments.

Gregory's relationship with Dorothy takes another step forward; only Gregory cannot see that it is only the football Dorothy is interested in. And at the same time, it becomes more and more apparent that Susan is falling for Gregory.

What is the difference between the girls when they are together and the boys when they are together? Complete these sentences and then write a paragraph about the differences.

The boys talk about . . .
The girls talk about . . .
The boys seem . . .
The girls seem . . .
The boys think . . .
The girls think . . .
The boys' attitude to girls is . . .
The girls' attitude to boys is . . .
The main difference between them is . . .
The main similarity between them is . . .

Section 2, *p. 95*

Gregory is over the moon. He wanders along beaming, which seriously alarms Miss Welch. He also notices Phil Menzies, pursuing Miss Welch, and realizes that the whole school is 'throbbing with romance' (p. 95). And he, too, is in love.

*

Gregory is becoming part of it all. No longer an outsider, he is joining the adult world. Notice how there is actually very little difference between Gregory and Phil; they are both concerned with sex, and unsure about it.

Section 3, *pp. 95–8*

Gregory accosts Steve by the boys' toilets, eager to tell him about his forthcoming meeting with Dorothy. Steve is far more interested in the cakes he's made, which are being sold in the toilets. He is still unwilling to lend Gregory his jacket for a date. In any case, Gregory hasn't actually got a date with Dorothy yet; as Steve points out, she only wants to play football with him. And last time Steve lent his jacket out, it came back covered with stains.

As he wanders round, collecting the takings from the cakes, Steve mellows, and agrees that if Gregory actually gets a date with Dorothy, then he can borrow the jacket.

Gregory is happy – until he passes another stall in the toilets and sees that the very same photo of Dorothy that he bought from Eric for twenty-five pence is being sold for ten pence. He snatches two extra copies to make up, and rushes off.

The wheels of romance are grinding into motion. Gregory is getting things organized: a jacket, and possibly shoes, from Steve. His hopes, and ours, are slowly building.

All this is set against a background of business. For lads like Steve (and Eric), unlike Gregory, are already hard at work, even though they haven't left school. Compared to Steve, Gregory is unemployed and immature.

Make a list of the differences between the two boys, using these headings.

Which boy do you admire most?
Which boy do you like most?
Which boy do you think will have the most successful future?

Section 4, *pp. 98–9*

Meanwhile, Andy is continuing to try to get a woman. He's been reading magazines, and worrying about not having made an approach to anyone.

So, with Charlie, he joins Margo and Carol at their table in the school canteen. The girls seem unimpressed, so Andy tries to involve them in conversation by telling them some particularly gory details about what they're eating. He's then surprised when both girls get up and leave.

Andy puts it all down to place; the desperate women he read about obviously didn't come from Scotland. Perhaps he and Charlie should go to South America, where there are eight women to every man.

The comedy of Andy trying to get a girl continues. What is he doing wrong in trying to chat the girls up? Do you blame the girls for reacting the way they do? What would you have done in their place? What does this scene show you about the differences between boys and girls?

Section 5, *pp. 100–101*

Gregory and Dorothy are playing football. Dorothy as usual is expert, scoring goal after goal as Gregory becomes more and more awkward.

He is happy, though, just to be with her; and any humiliation makes up for that. But as the practice continues, he begins to worry. Surely if it were an excuse to get off with him, Dorothy would be acting differently?

But he keeps going, complimenting Dorothy on her skill in a continuing attempt to get close to her. Dorothy starts to tease him, slamming goal after goal into the net, and sometimes into him. He sits down heavily, and breaks his neck chain.

Dorothy shows little sympathy. She just wants to get on with the game. Gregory starts to get really worried.

Very slowly, Gregory becomes aware of the real Dorothy behind the glamorous football player. He begins to suspect that his earlier hopes that she fancied him were incorrect. The real impact of her lack of sympathy won't hit him until much later, but already it has begun.

What do you think Dorothy is getting out of the practice? Does she really want to practise football, or is this the start of the plot dreamed up by Susan? How do you think Dorothy really thinks of Gregory?

Section 6, *pp. 101–2*

Andy is still trying. More of his inexpert lines, ending in a fascinating piece of information about sneezing, finally drive Susan away. Andy has failed again.

And he still doesn't know why. Read through all the references in the book to Andy and his attempts to get a woman. Then make a list of the things he's doing wrong. What would you advise him to do if you could talk to him?

CHAPTER 11

Section 1, *pp. 103–7*

Gregory and Dorothy have finished practising, and Gregory is un-happy. He is tired, hungry, sweaty and desperate – the hour is nearly over and all he and Dorothy have done is practise football together.

As they near the gym, Dorothy runs off to have a shower. Gregory is stunned, but then angry. He has to act. He runs after Dorothy desperately, and catches up with her at the gym.

'. . . would you like to come out with me?' (p. 104). To his total amazement, Dorothy agrees. He repeats the question, twice more, and she still agrees! She states a time and place for them to meet, and disappears into the changing room.

Gregory is wildly happy – so wildly happy that Phil Menzies, who has been watching them, thinks the worst. He knocks, and goes into the girls' changing room to check that Dorothy is all right.

She is fine, but once in the changing room, Phil decides to talk. Dorothy realizes that she should make peace with Phil, for her own sake. She thanks him for having her in the team. Phil is equally grateful to her, and they begin to talk.

Dorothy is genuinely interested in how to improve her game. Phil, unused to such intelligent enthusiasm, is keen to help. He coaches her, at first dramatically, then with increasing enthusiasm. Dorothy is impressed, following Phil's coaching expertly and gratefully. Phil is impressed by her skill, her style, the way she follows his coaching. We leave them together, happy and united in one love – football.

In this section, Gregory finally asks Dorothy out, and gets a positive reply. What makes him ask? What finally drives him to action? And how is this a change for Gregory?

In fact, we are probably aware that there is something not quite right about Dorothy's acceptance. She doesn't really want to go out with Gregory. But we don't yet know what is going on.

Then Phil Menzies enters. For the first time, he and Dorothy communicate. What do you think each of them is thinking and feeling during this scene? Pretend you are Phil, talking to his mates in the pub afterwards, and describing what happened, how his attitude towards Dorothy suddenly changed. Write about the conversation. How do you think he will treat Dorothy in future? And how do you think Dorothy will react to him? Has Dorothy now finally proved that she is as good, if not better, at football than the boys?

Section 2, *pp. 107–8*

At home that evening, Gregory prepares to go out. Madeleine is helping, excited and supportive. After his bath, she dries his hair for him, maternally.

Gregory is still concerned about what to talk about – and he and Madeleine giggle at the thought of telling Dorothy a dirty joke. Gregory eyes his new clothes and Steve's jacket, and is happy.

*

Have you or any of your friends ever been out on a first date? If so, how did you feel? Look at the way Gregory obviously feels, and make notes on that. Then compare it with how you or your friends felt. Did you have someone to share it with, as Gregory has Madeleine? What does the way they interact together show us about their relationship?

CHAPTER 12

Section 1, *pp. 109–13*

A quarter of an hour after Dorothy is due to arrive at the rendezvous, there is no sign of her. Gregory feels terrible. His feelings have changed from one emotion to another throughout the evening, and now he is at an all-time low.

Then, suddenly, he hears the sound of footsteps. He is sure it is Dorothy, and turns away nonchalantly to look into a window. When he turns round, it is Carol.

She tells Gregory that Dorothy isn't coming. Shocked beyond belief, at first he cannot react. Then, as Carol keeps talking, telling him that Dorothy is doing something else, asking him about his coat, he slowly starts to react to her. He asks if she'd like to go for a walk with him.

She agrees, and his spirits rise immediately. They decide to go up to the fish and chip shop. Gregory consoles himself that at least he has a date. Then he realizes that Carol has disappeared into a telephone box, and is changing her clothes. She makes him stand with his back to the door to hide her. When she re-emerges, she is dressed as a punk – to Gregory's total embarrassment.

He tries to escape, but Carol angrily pushes him towards the chip shop.

Gregory is stood up. In fact, he is being prepared for a much nicer treat than Dorothy, but he doesn't realize this. He only knows that she hasn't turned up. His emotions swing this way and that. Read the section through and write down all the emotions that Gregory experiences. If you've ever been stood up, you might compare how he feels to the way you felt. And how does he feel, and react, when Carol changes into her punk clothes?

Now think about Carol. What sort of person is she? Why do you think she changes her clothes in the telephone box? Do you think she's being nasty to Gregory when she gets angry with him, or is she actually helping him?

Section 2, *pp. 113–16*

At the chip shop, Gregory is embarrassed to find Andy and Charlie; he's sure they're watching him scornfully.

He feels even worse when Carol tells him that Dorothy 'knows' (p. 114) (Does she mean 'is going out with'?) a boy at the physical ed. college who is nineteen and has a car. He replies with sarcasm, to hide the envy he feels, that he has been 'defeated by sheer age' (p. 114).

Carol, though, is about to leave; she already has a date and is handing Gregory over to Margo. Gregory is even more confused – but at least Margo isn't punk. He passes the time when she is buying chips by chatting to Andy and Charlie, suggesting that Margo fancies him.

Led off again by Margo, who has just made a phone call while in the chip shop, Gregory is bemused. Andy is envious.

The plot thickens. Gregory now has no idea of what is going on, as he is passed from girl to girl. Notice how Margo makes a phone call (Who to? Saying what?) and thus moves the plan on a stage further.

Now it is Gregory who is the envy of his friends, and Andy who has become what Gregory was at the start of the book – the outsider, not allowed into the secrets of boy–girl relationships. Gregory, though totally controlled, is at least being led in the right direction.

Section 3, *pp. 116–17*

Gregory and Margo walk along together, but Gregory is beginning to rethink his theory that Margo is after him. At first she doesn't talk and, even when she does tell him to relax, she doesn't want him to put his arm round her waist. He suspects he is 'a lamb en route to some bizarre kind of slaughter' (p. 117); at any rate it is a totally new experience for him.

The tension builds, for Gregory and for us, as he is passed from hand to hand. All the girls know what is going on, all of them are determined to push Gregory in the right direction. They are in total control – and Gregory can only go along with it.

Section 4, *pp. 117–18*

Meanwhile, Susan is waiting. She has received the message from Margo to say that Gregory is coming, and she is dressed up ready to meet him. She particularly likes the beret, a touch of style perched on the back of her head.

She wonders how Gregory will react. She isn't worried by the thought of his reaction, just concerned to make him notice her. After all, she cares for him, which is more than Dorothy does.

As she looks, Margo and Gregory appear.

We realize here for the first time, though we may have suspected it, that it is Susan who has laid this trap for Gregory. She has seen him, wanted him, and has now set out to get him.

Read the section through. It's the first time we have really understood how Susan's mind works. What do you learn from her thoughts as she stands waiting?

Section 5, *pp. 118–25*

Gregory doesn't notice Susan at first, then is quite impressed with her. Before he can start to react, Margo has announced that she is off, and he is left with Susan. He is confused.

Susan is very direct; she asks Gregory whether he'd like a date with her. He slowly begins to understand what has happened when she tells him that girls 'help each other' (p. 119). Then he needs time to think.

He wonders whether to feel hurt, but really he feels flattered that someone feels strongly enough about him to go to all this trouble. As he looks over at Susan, he begins to rethink things: she's attractive, well-dressed, fanciable in fact. And she likes him. He agrees to a date with her.

The two of them set off for the country park; thoughts of lust and passion cross Gregory's mind, but he soon realizes that he is just quite comfortable in Susan's company. They talk, walk, whistle and grin at each other. And it is all very easy – almost like being with his male friends.

Unnoticed by Gregory, Andy and Charlie see him heading for the park with Susan. Andy is overcome with envy.

Gregory and Susan, in the country park, are sitting on the grass and talking happily. Gregory shows her how to 'dance' lying down (p. 122), and tells her all about clinging to the surface of the earth. Their happiness is interrupted only by Eric, who is hung about with camera equipment, and is off to the nurses' home to take pictures. Gregory isn't interested in that any more.

Nor is he really interested in Dorothy. He realizes that Susan is fun – something Dorothy isn't. Then he forgets about Dorothy again, for good.

At last, it is time for Gregory to go home. Susan walks him to his door, their arms linked, then around each other's waists.

At last, easily and naturally, Gregory finds a girl. Or rather, she finds him. Susan takes him over from Margo, suggests a date, then lets their natural compatibility take over. And it is all easy, not difficult like it was with Dorothy, to talk, walk and finally touch.

What changes do you see in Gregory during this scene? What does he learn, what knowledge and what skills? How does he change, in himself? And what about Susan – does she change, or is she just being herself? Make a list of the differences between the way the two of them handle the situation.

Do you think they are suitable for each other? Was Susan right to 'set Gregory up' for this date as she does? Would he have been happier continuing to dream of Dorothy?

Why do you think the scene includes Andy and Eric? What do these two show about Gregory, and about the whole business of relationships between boys and girls?

Section 6, *pp. 125–8*

At Gregory's door, they kiss, again and again. They share secret jokes, laughs, and hugs. It is all very easy and happy. They arrange to meet in school the next day, and Gregory suddenly wants to be alone, really to feel this totally new sensation of romance.

In fact, they've not been alone, for Madeleine has been at the window above, unable to hear but eager to know what is going on. She hears Gregory come upstairs, and then go into his room and turn off the light.

When, wild with curiosity, she goes in to him, he is fully dressed and lying on his bed bemused. She questions him fiercely, and he tells her everything, or almost. She challenges him when he denies kissing Susan, and Gregory is scared in case she wakes their parents.

Finally, Madeleine kisses Gregory lightly, and asks, 'Who's going to be Gregory's girl . . .?' To which he replies 'You are!' (p. 128).

When Madeleine has gone, Gregory is left with his own thoughts. He cannot believe that he ever felt anything for Dorothy, when Susan is so friendly and sympathetic – and makes him feel like this.

He settles down in bed, and smiles to himself. He is happy.

Finally, Gregory and Susan get to kiss. It is much easier, and far more delightful than he ever dreamed possible, full of little giggles and shared jokes. And afterwards – how do you think Gregory really feels?

What about Susan; how do you think she feels as she walks home? What does she tell her friends the next day?

The two of them arrange to meet. Do you think they will go out together? What sort of relationship will they have, and how long will it last? Will they settle down together, or will this be the first of a number of relationships that each of them has?

Look at the way the book ends, with Gregory returning home to

Madeleine. Has his relationship with her changed? What does he mean when he says that it is she who is Gregory's girl?

Notice the last words of the book. They are the words that began the book – what does that mean, and what is it meant to show us about Gregory?

Finally, take a broad view of the book. Did you like it? Did you, if you have seen it, like the film on which the book is based? What criticisms would you make of either the film or the book?

Write a review of the book, or the film, as if you were a newspaper critic. Say what you liked about it, and what didn't work for you. What would make you recommend it to other people, and what would make you advise them against it? How could it be improved?

If you were able to talk to Bill Forsyth, what would you say to him about *Gregory's Girl*?

Characters

GREGORY

Gregory is the central focus of the book. He starts it, he finishes it, and he and his concerns, thoughts and emotions run all the way through the book.

But what sort of person is he? Like all the other characters, he is Scottish. He is sixteen, growing fast, still spotty and only just beginning to shave. What else can you say about what Gregory looks like?

Next, think about his background. Where does he live, what sort of family does he come from, what sort of education is he getting? List the subjects you know he is taking at school, and think about what they tell you about him.

What is Gregory's personality like? Mark on this chart what sort of a person he seems to you by circling the number on the scale 1–5 that seems most appropriate.

Shy	1	2	3	4	5	Out-going
Intellectual	1	2	3	4	5	Un-intellectual
Kind	1	2	3	4	5	Unkind
Unsure of himself	1	2	3	4	5	Confident
Effective	1	2	3	4	5	Ineffectual
Humorous	1	2	3	4	5	No sense of humour
Gentle	1	2	3	4	5	Aggressive
Decisive	1	2	3	4	5	Indecisive
Confused	1	2	3	4	5	Certain
Aware	1	2	3	4	5	Unaware

Do you agree with Gordon-John Sinclair that Gregory is actually 'a looney . . . totally mad'? What do you think Gregory himself would say to this comment?

Look, too, at what Gregory's thoughts and opinions are. What does he think about the important issues that are raised in the book? Make notes on Gregory's thoughts on the following topics:

The differences between boys and girls
Equal opportunites
Sex
Love
Romance
Marriage
Having a family
Education
Going to work
Friendship
Mixing with other people
Growing up

What does Gregory think about other people, and how do they react to him? First, how does Gregory get on with his own family? We don't see much of his parents, but you can tell something of how he gets on with them.

We see much more of how he gets on with Madeleine, and we can tell a lot about Gregory from the way he treats his sister, and the way she reacts to him. Look particularly at the fact that she supports him in finding a girlfriend. Who, in the end, does he choose as 'Gregory's girl'?

What about Gregory's friends? Do they get on with him – is he the leader, or one of the group? And do they respect him or admire him?

How does he behave towards them, think about them, feel about them? In particular, what about the friends who have left school, gone to work, plan to marry? What does Gregory need from his friends? Does he get it, or not? Do you think Gregory will keep in touch with his friends when he leaves school, and, if so, which ones?

Gregory's teachers vary from regarding him with amazement to finding him quite off-putting. Phil Menzies avoids him in the corridor, Miss Ford teases him. Write a school report for Gregory, with comments from Phil, Miss Welch and the domestic science teacher. What do you think they say about him in the report; what judgements do they make about him? How do you think they regard him in private?

Girls, mostly, don't think much of Gregory. The 5A group think he's a 'wally' (p. 56). Why do you imagine they feel that? Susan is the only one who sees anything in him, and he doesn't even notice her for most of the book. What do you think Susan sees in Gregory?

And what do you think Gregory sees in Dorothy? Dorothy is the person whom Gregory worships, and it is his passion for Dorothy that is the focal point of the book.

Gregory develops through this passion. He changes, from the vague readiness of the first chapter to someone who acts. Look carefully at the way Gregory behaves when he falls for Dorothy. Read over again the passages after he first sees her (pp. 43–52), and begin to chart the various emotions that he feels. What are they?

Certainly, Gregory feels sexually attracted to Dorothy, although he never seems to imagine making love with her. He also claims to be in love with her, and expects her to respond to that. Do you think he really is in love? What evidence have you got? One thing is certain: Dorothy and Gregory will never have a relationship. Even with all the sympathy in the world for Gregory, we cannot see the two of them as a partnership. Why?

In the end, Dorothy does not care for Gregory. Gregory fools himself that he has a chance with her for far too long. Then he begins to realize that there is someone who does care for him and, as he does so, he changes again.

With Susan, Gregory begins to grow up. He starts to relax, and to forget about putting on a show. He begins to enjoy sexuality, to enjoy being himself. He likes Susan, in a way that he never liked Dorothy, not because she is a fantasy, but because she makes him laugh, because she has style, because everything is easy when he is with her (p. 120). And, for Gregory, this is a step forward.

Make a list of the ways in which Gregory changes through the book, first by falling for Dorothy, and then by going out with Susan. Can you remember, or imagine yourself, changing in the same sort of ways when you first had a crush on someone, and first had a relationship with someone?

The most vital thing about Gregory is his character and the way he responds and interacts with other people. He shows us, as no other character in the book does, the main messages of the book. His trials and tribulations take us deeply into the experience of being sixteen and not knowing anyone of the opposite sex. He shows us how difficult it is to grow up, how hard it is to reconcile the pull of wanting to go out to work and yet wanting to stay in the safety of school. He shows us what agony it is to feel sexual and not have had sexual experience – and how much more fun it is, often, to forget about sex and to talk and laugh instead.

Make notes on what Gregory shows us under these headings. Then write a paragraph on each, explaining how Gerald Cole uses Gregory to give us the central message of his book.

Growing up
Education
Sexuality
Love
Romance
Girls and boys

What, in fact, do you think will happen to Gregory? Will his relationship with Susan last and, if so, for how long? Do you agree with Gordon John Sinclair that Gregory and Susan will 'probably get married when they're twenty'? Will Gregory settle down to schoolwork, pass his exams? Will he find his form again in football, or will that now become unimportant to him, as his interests go elsewhere?

What will Gregory be like as an adult – will he find a job, settle down, get married? What sort of a father will he be? And will he look back, amused, at the way he used to feel about all the things he now takes for granted – work, sex, relationships?

Finally, ask yourself whether you like Gregory. Do you agree with Dorothy that he is a 'wally' (p. 56), or with Susan and Madeleine who admire and care for him? Do you see anything of yourself in Gregory as he grows up? If you were rewriting *Gregory's Girl*, would you change Gregory in any way – or keep him just as he is?

DOROTHY

Dorothy is Gregory's flesh-and-blood dream. From ogling nurses and fancying bus drivers, Gregory moves on to falling for a real, attainable girl, who stirs his blood and is skilled at the sport that he loves – Dorothy.

How does Gregory see Dorothy? He certainly thinks she is beautiful, he definitely admires her football skill. Go through the book, noticing the way he thinks, speaks, dreams and fantasizes about her, and then make notes under these headings:

What Gregory thinks and feels about Dorothy's appearance.
What he thinks and feels about her personality.
What he thinks and feels about her as a footballer.

Part of the attraction for Gregory is that Dorothy combines the two great interests of his life – sex and football. As Gordon-John Sinclair commented in the interview at the start of the book, 'a girl who can play football . . . what more can you want?' He's not ready to forsake the game yet to go after girls. He needs someone who represents both.

And so Dorothy takes over Gregory's life. What effect does she have on him? Make a list of all the changes that occur in Gregory, all the things he does just because of Dorothy. Which of these are rational and beneficial? Which of them do you think are silly?

The one thing that Gregory doesn't do is relate to Dorothy as a person. For what is she really like? Look back at the notes that you made on the way Gregory sees Dorothy. How many of the judgements he makes about her are true, and how many are his imagination? What sort of girl is she really? Is she a '*femme fatale*' as Gordon John Sinclair suggested?

Read back over the sections where Dorothy appears. What is she like? What are her interests, and her attitudes? How does she treat other people, those from whom she wants something (like Gordon), and those who want something from her?

What is Dorothy's main interest? Is she good at football, and what does this tell us about her? Certainly, she is committed to the game (Can you give examples of this?) and does well in the team. The one time she really shows life and enthusiasm is when she learns a good football move from Phil Menzies.

How does Dorothy treat Gregory? She knows he's keen on her; how does she know? When she realizes, how does she react, and does her attitude to Gregory alter? On the other hand, does she lead him on – and how does she, in the end, help him to get what is best for him? Think about Gordon-John Sinclair's comments in the interview that it is not Dorothy's fault that Gregory falls for her, or that she doesn't fall for him. Do you agree with this opinion? If not, why not?

Imagine you are Dorothy, writing a letter to a friend, or a diary entry, about the time from the day you get accepted in the football team to the day Susan comes into school to say that she went out with Gregory. What would your version of the whole story be?

You might like to consider whether you like Dorothy and, as a separate question, whether you admire her. The message is, as Gregory realizes in the end, that she's not the girl for him. But you might find some things in her that make you respect and admire her. What might these be?

She is crucial to the book. She is the focus of Gregory's attention, his fantasies, his dreams. She represents everything that he wants. She also represents the strong, effective woman who is as good as – even better than – the men, who is mature and sexual and totally 'together'. However much we sympathize with Gregory, we have to admit that he's not up to Dorothy.

What else does Dorothy do in the book? She shows us the characters of most of the other people in it, particularly the men. Make a list of how these people show their characters in responding to Dorothy:

Gordon
Phil Menzies
Steve
The other girls

Finally, notice how, unlike most of the other people in the book, Dorothy doesn't seem to be a humorous character. She never slips up, seldom shows a humorous side, and is far too together to be the butt of a joke, as many of the men in the book are. Why do you think this is?

Dorothy, then, isn't Gregory's girl, nor will she ever be. But she is crucial to the book, and to Gregory. Through her, he grows, develops and learns that the dream is not the reality – and is not nearly as good as the reality, either.

MADELEINE

Madeleine is Gregory's girl. He says so at the end of the book (p. 128). What do you think he means by it – in what way is his sister Gregory's girl?

Along with Dorothy and Susan, Madeleine is one of the most important girls in the book. What do you know about her? Can you complete these sentences with facts about Madeleine?

Madeleine is . . . years old.
She has . . . hair.
She goes to the . . . school near . . . .
Madeleine enjoys eating . . . .
She enjoys drinking . . . .
She likes spending her time . . . .

What sort of a person is Madeleine? Make a list of words you would use to describe her. Then write about her character. Is she sensible or silly, hard-hearted or kind?

In particular, think about the way she relates to the people she meets. Think about how she behaves to these people: Richard, Billy, the waitress in the cafe. What does the way she behaves and what she says show us about her? Think, too, about the people in her life we don't know anything about; we don't see Madeleine with her parents, with teachers, or with girlfriends (Do you imagine she has any?).

The main relationship we see Madeleine in is the one she has with Gregory. What do you think she feels about him? Read through all the scenes in the book where Madeleine is with Gregory, and the places in the book where Gregory thinks about Madeleine. Then write two paragraphs, one about Gregory as if you were Madeleine, and one about Madeleine as if you were Gregory. What do you imagine they would say about each other?

We learn a lot from Madeleine, not only about Gregory but also about the differences between boys and girls. Like all the girls in the book, she is shown as very self-confident and self-possessed. How does this compare with Gregory? Does Madeleine realize this? What does she think about boys in general, and Gregory in particular?

In fact, in many ways Madeleine helps Gregory to get a girl. How? Some sisters can be jealous of their brother's girlfriends. Do you think Madeleine is? Think about the way she reacts to Dorothy, and also about the way she reacts at the end of the book after Gregory has been kissing Susan. What do you think she feels then?

Madeleine also shows us that being grown-up is nothing to do with age. She is much younger than Gregory, but in many ways she is much more mature than he is. Make a list of the ways in which Madeleine behaves in a more adult way than Gregory. Do you think she will carry on being grown-up even when she reaches adolescence?

Finally, look at Madeleine's views and insights on romance and sex. She isn't supposed to know about sex, but in fact she does, although she makes it very clear that she is far too young to do so. She also knows all about romance, and gives Gregory very good advice. Do you think Madeleine has a romance with Richard?

When thinking about Madeleine as a character in the book, be very aware of why she is there. She isn't just Gregory's sister. She also represents many things that are good about strong, effective, mature women, even though she is only ten. And she shows us a great deal about Gregory. She gives him a lot of support, is the most stable female in his life, and will probably outlast Susan, let alone Dorothy.

For all these reasons – and you can probably add more of your own – Madeleine is 'Gregory's girl'.

SUSAN

Although it is Madeleine whom Gregory calls his 'girl', it is Susan who ends up as Gregory's girlfriend.

At first we, like Gregory, see very little of her. She is one of Dorothy's crowd, and not the most glamorous of them.

But, slowly, we begin to realize that she likes Gregory. He reminds her of an ostrich (p. 56), and she is a girl who likes ostriches (pp. 89, 118). She is aware enough to realize that he likes Dorothy, whom she admires; but she is also self-confident enough to go for Gregory herself, and trust that he will in the end prefer her to Dorothy.

She's right. She mounts a complicated plot to get Gregory, and when she does, he falls hook, line and sinker. When he gets to know her, Gregory much prefers the stylish, down-to-earth Susan, who whistles with him and dances lying down. We, like Gregory, learn more about Susan in the last chapter of the book than in all the previous chapters; and what we know, we like.

Susan is important to Gregory, not just at the end of the book when he is falling in love with her, but all through it. For it is Susan who is the real person, not the ideal; Susan who cares for Gregory rather than mocking him. As Gordon-John Sinclair commented, Susan and Gregory are 'on the same wavelength'.

Find out about Susan. What does she look like, what sort of clothes does she wear? Who are her friends – and why does she hang around with that particular group? What are her interests, what does she study?

And what sort of person is she? Read the last chapter of the book carefully, and then make a list of words you could use to describe Susan; write a description of her as you see her.

Susan wins, Dorothy is relegated to nowhere in Gregory's mind. And they are very different people. Gregory points out that Dorothy is 'hard . . . unyielding . . . unsympathetic' (p. 128), and infers that Susan isn't. In what other ways are they different? Make a full list of the similarities and differences between Dorothy and Susan under these headings:

Looks
Age
Intelligence
Outside interests
Sense of humour
Self-confidence
Self-awareness

Selfishness
Sexuality
Practicality
Ability to go for what she wants
Successfulness

Which girl do you prefer? Which would you make a friend of, and which do you think would make a better intimate partner? Do you think Gregory has got the best deal?

But, Susan isn't only in the book as the girl who gets Gregory. There are other reasons for her being there. At the start, and for quite a way through the book, she is just one of the 'gaol-bait 5A' (p. 41), friends and supporters of Dorothy. She also interacts with other characters, like Steve and Andy, to show us things about them.

Perhaps most importantly, she shows us what girls can be like at sixteen, in comparison with what boys are like. Susan is mature, knows what she wants and is effective in getting it. She is relaxed with Gregory and makes him feel at ease. She is happy to let things happen without pushing them, to appreciate Gregory for what he is and to enjoy being with him, rather than rushing into sex or backing away from a friendship. She seems far more mature than Gregory in many ways, just as many of the girls in the book seem more mature than the boys.

She may not be Gregory's girlfriend for ever, but Susan certainly deserves to have him, and to keep him for a long while. Do you think she will? Do you, like Gordon-John Sinclair, think that Susan and Gregory are 'right for each other'?

PHIL MENZIES

Of all the teachers, Phil Menzies is the one whose character we see most of. What sort of person is he?

Make notes about Phil under these headings, looking through the book and collecting incidents and quotations to back up your answers:

His appearance
His job
His attitude to his job
His outside interests
His attitude to women and sex
His attitude to Gregory
His personality

You should now be getting a fairly full picture of the sort of person Phil is. Now look at the role he plays in the book.

What is he there for? Certainly, his own character is clear, and adds to the impact of the book. We see him as a real person, and we know what he feels and thinks.

He also shows us a lot about other people. Read through the sections where he meets Gregory, and notice how Gregory reacts when he is with Phil, how we learn more about Gregory through these meetings.

Look at the way Phil interacts with Dorothy. Her character, her self-containment, show through at the football trials (pp. 41–6), and when he is teaching her a new football pass (pp. 105–7) we see her in a totally new light.

We see through Phil that although Gregory may not be totally together over women, romance and sex, neither is Phil. He is just as uncertain as Gregory is, even though he's a lot older. Think back to your answers to the questions about Gregory on pages 49–52. Who is the more mature, Phil or Gregory?

Phil shows us a lot about education. He is the most developed of the teacher characters, and as we see him interact with the other staff, feeling put down by some, being scared by the Headmaster, lusting after the female members of staff, we see a sympathetic if caricatured figure of a teacher. Do you think he's a good teacher? Write two paragraphs, one arguing that he is, one arguing that he isn't. Which argument seems strongest to you?

Finally, Phil Menzies adds to the humour of the book. As you read through the incidents where he appears, notice how funny he is, with his self-deception, his nervousness, the way he is made a fool of by Dorothy and sometimes even by Gregory. We don't laugh at him, we often laugh with him; nevertheless, Phil is a humorous character.

THE GIRLS

Who are Dorothy's friends, the girls of 5A? First of all, make sure you know who they are. Then gather some general information about them. They are all in the fifth year, so are probably between fifteen and seventeen years old. What do they look like? How do they dress? What are they like as people?

The girls, apart from Dorothy and Susan, are not clearly developed as characters. They are representative of 'girls in general', as they are shown in this book. Choose from this list the words that you think best describe them:

Attractive
Unsure
Capable
Intelligent
Skilful
Confused
Direct
Effective
Confident
Sexually experienced

Now go through the book looking for references to the girls. Look especially at chapter 12, at the way in which the girls lead Gregory to Susan.

What sort of people are these fifth-form girls shown to be? How do they behave with each other? How do they relate to teachers? To men? How do you think they behave when they are with their families?

How do other people relate to them? Why do you think the teachers are wary? Why do Gregory and his friends treat them with awe?

Do you think these girls are the same on the inside as they are on the outside, or are they different? How do you imagine them to think and feel when they are alone?

What is the role of the girls in the book – what are they there for? Think about the times they appear, like a chorus supporting Dorothy, then Susan. What do they do? What do they achieve in the book?

What do they show us of other people – particularly members of their own group, and members of the opposite sex? How are they different from the boys in the way they react, talk, approach things? What is the book trying to say about what girls are like as people?

One thing the girls don't do is take a large role in the humorous parts of the book. That is left to Gregory and his male friends. Why do you think this is? What is the book trying to say by not making the girls so much of a joke as the boys are?

Finally, think about the girls you know who are the same age as Margo, Liz, Carol. Are they the same or different? So, do you think that the way these girls are shown in the book is realistic? And does this way of presenting the girls work for you?

THE TEACHERS

The teachers at Climackton Comprehensive seem ordinary and real. Only Phil Menzies is explored in detail. The others, Alec Wilson, Alistair Stewart, Miss Ford, the Italian teacher, Miss Welch, the English teacher, and the Evil Swine, the Headmaster, are mentioned briefly and in little depth. But, together, they give us the impression of a mixed bunch, as found in any school, of people who have real faults, real virtues and who are, above all, very human.

Alec Wilson, the senior biology master, is the sort of teacher young girls get crushes on. He shows us the danger of not being able to handle it. Alistair Stewart has compromised his specialization in history to teach a more highly paid subject, and it depresses him. Miss Ford teaches a minority subject, and is always looking for extra pupils, but she can still recognize that Gregory doesn't want to do Italian because he loves the language – and can tease him about it.

Miss Welch, nickname Raquel, is outgoing enough and mature enough to be able to respond as an adult to an ex-student who is now working in an adult world. How does this ex-student (Billy) respond to her?

Finally, the Evil Swine, who puts the fear of everything into his staff, is able to negotiate shrewdly with a fifth-former (Steve) for a good tea for the Parent–Teacher Association. That same fifth-former respects and admires him as an equal, while his staff quake in their shoes.

Which of the teachers at Climackton do you most recognize? Are there any that are like teachers at your school or college? Choose one of them and imagine you are that teacher. What would you say about the school, about the pupils and about the other staff? What would you say in particular about Gregory, Dorothy, Susan and the other students mentioned in the book?

Do you feel the teachers at Climackton Comprehensive are good teachers? How could they improve? What advice would you give them if you met them?

What function do the teachers fulfil in the book? They are all interesting, but very minor, characters, appearing briefly to provide a background to what is happening to Gregory. What do they add to the book, to the film, by being there? What do they show us of Gregory, and of the other main characters? What do they show us of the main issues explored? How do they add to the humour?

If you were rewriting the book, or remaking the film, how would you portray the teachers from Climackton Comprehensive?

THE BOYS

Gregory's Girl is not just about Gregory and his struggle to get a girlfriend. It is about all boys his age, and how they cope with the trials and tribulations of growing up, getting on with the opposite sex, and easing their way into the adult world.

So, we see a whole variety of lads of Gregory's age, some in school and some out, some with girlfriends, some without. All of them show us something about what it is like to be a boy, and so all of them show us something about Gregory.

To start with, look through the book and see how many boys you can find mentioned. You should find at least seven mentioned by name. Now think about which of them fall into these categories:

Which boys go to school?
Which boys are at work?

Which boys find it easy to get on with girls?
Which boys are desperate to find a girlfriend?
Which boys are more interested in business?
Which boys play football?

You should have realized by now that we see a cross-section of boys in the book; some of them are caricatures, most are portrayals of true elements of all teenage boys. Many of them, like Gregory, are shy, have spots, are only just shaving, worry about sex. Some of them, like Gordon, seem very confident and unworried, successful in a lot of what they do.

Gregory's particular friend is Steve. He is an expert chef, and an excellent entrepreneur, thoroughly enjoying the cut and thrust of negotiating with the Headmaster. Although still at school, he is already a businessman. What else do you know about him? What are his opinions about sex, about girls, about his future life? And how do you think he will do in his future life – will he be successful, what will his lifestyle be? Notice how Steve is Dorothy's counterpart: successful, attractive, yet actually far more interested in what he is good at. Notice, too, that while Dorothy is good at a 'man's game'. Steve's expertise is in a 'woman's craft'.

Another of Gregory's friends is Eric. He is keen on photography, but, unlike Steve's cookery, it seems for Eric to be a substitute for real life. When Gregory is with Susan, Eric is far more interested in taking photos of women than of the real thing. He is also a businessman, overcharging Gregory for the photos. How do you think Eric will make out later on in life?

Andy is the comic figure of the group, almost a caricature of the overeager boy who tries to chat up girls and gets it horribly wrong. Read over the scenes he appears in, and notice how through the book his little story unfolds as he gets more and more desperate to get a woman. Eventually, he is in anguish as he watches Gregory with his third woman of the night. How does Andy's story add to the humour of the book?

Charlie, Andy's mate, says nothing, because he is too thoughtful, too shy or too dim. Another of Gregory's friends, Pete, is also a shadowy figure, popping in and out of the football scene.

Outside school, firmly in the world of work, are Billy and Gary.

Billy represents the lad who has left school and is enjoying all the benefits: a steady job, nice clothes, lots of money and free time. He lords it over the others when they come out of school. What do you think he is meant to show, in comparison to Gregory? What is he meant to make us realize about the grown-up world outside school?

The even more grown-up world is represented by Gary. Not only does he have a job, but he is about to get married with a child on the way. Gregory sees this as enviable; do you agree? Do you think Gary knows what he is doing, taking on a family at sixteen – do you think he will regret it? How do you think Gregory would cope if the same thing happened to him?

Gary also represents a much more experienced sexuality than Gregory's. Where Gregory has had a peck on the cheek, Gary has slept with his girlfriend. What does this show us about sexuality at this stage in a person's life – and what does it show us about Gregory?

Of all the boys individually, who seems to you to be the most interesting? Once you have decided, go back and read the sections where he appears, and gather as much information about him as you can. Find out about his appearance, if possible, his character, his ideas and views. What does he spend his time doing? What is important to him? Then ask yourself what his role is in the book – what does he show us or tell us about the main characters? What does he tell us about the main issues in the book? Does he add humour, or a touch of seriousness to what is going on? Does he make us, or Gregory, stop and think?

Now, write three paragraphs about him: one as if you were Gregory, talking about his friend; one as if you were a teacher/ex-teacher of the boy; one paragraph as if you were the boy talking about himself.

Finally, look at the boys as a group. What do they add to the book? What do they tell us about growing up just by being there, presenting us with all the different facets of growing up as a boy? If you had been the author, would you have left any one of them out; or would you have added any other boy, to show us another aspect of maleness?

RICHARD

We meet Madeleine's friend Richard at about the same time as we meet Madeleine; he wants to walk her home after school while she is waiting for Gregory (pp. 78–9). Later in the day he calls to take her for a walk and is driven away by Gregory (pp. 86–8).

What do you know about Richard? Make a list of the things you learn about his appearance, his age, the sort of person he is. How does Madeleine see him? What does Gregory think of him?

But his main reasons for being in the book are not to do with his own character, but what he shows us of other people, and of the ideas in the book. What does Richard show us about Madeleine? What does he show us about Gregory, both in comparison with the older boy, and in the way Gregory treats him when he meets him?

Think about what Richard is meant to show us about how some young people, especially youngsters of that age, treat relationships with the opposite sex. Who is he meant to be compared with in this?

Finally, think about what Richard shows us about what growing up means.

MR AND MRS UNDERWOOD

Gregory's mum and dad must be important as they brought Gregory up and made him what he is. But we see almost nothing of them. Mrs Underwood we don't meet, and only hear about briefly.

Mr Underwood appears when he meets Gregory on his way to school and teases him about their never actually having any contact. He seems a gentle, kindly man, genuinely fond of Gregory and Madeleine. Certainly, he is sure, and right to be sure, that Gregory is not a vandal (pp. 30–1); therefore he must have brought him up well.

We know very little, too, about Gregory's attitude to his parents. He seems to live his life apart from them, working out his own ideas without consulting them, concerned only not to wake them up by being too noisy, not to worry them unduly.

Why do you think Mr and Mrs Underwood are hardly mentioned in the book? Is this deliberate, or not? If it is deliberate, think of some reasons why they are excluded – what does it do for the book, what does it show about Gregory, the life he leads, the stage he is at, the way he is growing up?

Themes

EDUCATION

It is no coincidence that most of the book *Gregory's Girl* is set in Gregory's school. School life, and the education system, are one of the main focal points of interest in the book. Why do you think this is? What is so interesting about education?

First, since Gregory doesn't play truant, he spends most of every day at school. Most of the things that interest him in life are there – his friends, his football, even the exams which he's not too sure whether he wants to take. So school is important to Gregory; and whether the school, and the education system as a whole, work for him seems to be important to the book.

Look first at the school, Climackton Comprehensive, itself. What do you know about it? Look back over the descriptions of the buildings, the area in which it is set, and find out what you can. Build up a picture of it, a neighbourhood comprehensive with the primary school next door, to which all the young people in the area go.

What about the staff? You might like to read over the part of the section on Characters which deals with the staff, and remind yourself who they are. Answer these questions to refresh your memory.

Who is the English teacher? Who does she chat to in an English lesson?
What hobbies does the P E teacher have? Who does he fancy?
Who is the senior biology master?
Who teaches religion even though it isn't his subject?
What is the Head's nickname?
Who is the Italian teacher?

Now think more broadly about these teachers, and the way they teach. What would you expect from a good teacher? Think of any good teachers you've ever known, and remember what they were like. Then make a list of the things you might expect a good teacher to do, or to feel:

Try to help?
Keep good discipline?
Be understanding?

Go through the list of teachers, particularly the ones we know most about, like Miss Welch and Phil Menzies. Compare them with the list you have made. Would you say they were good teachers? Do they live up to your expectations?

How could the teachers in Gregory's school do better – could they be more aware, or less involved? In particular, look at how they treat boys as opposed to girls, and vice versa. Do they give them equal opportunities, do they develop them to their full potential regardless of their gender? Could they treat Gregory, or Dorothy, or Susan, in a better way?

Having looked at the school, and the teachers, look at what the school experience is actually doing for Gregory and the other young people. Look at these sentences. Which do you think are the closest approximations to what the young people really feel about school?

They hate school and miss it when they can.
They tolerate school and find some good things in it.
They wouldn't miss school for anything.
They realize they must stay at school if they want to get anywhere in
    life.
They quite enjoy school for the social life.
They value the teachers and think they do their best.
They humour the teachers and put up with them.
They consider the teachers to be totally misguided.

Write a paragraph as if you were Gregory, saying what you think and feel about education in general and your school in particular. Suggest ways the school could improve.

In fact, Gregory does consider leaving school. When? And for what reasons? What is it that tempts Gregory to leave school and try to make his way in the big wide world; what rewards would make him go to work?

On the other hand, in many ways, school for Gregory is a retreat, a way to hide from the responsibilities that Gary and Billy have. He quite likes the easy life, the ability to be able to get up late and saunter into class, the freedom to sort himself out in his own time without having to worry about anything.

For some of Gregory's friends, school is not such an easy option. Steve, for example, is actually running his own little business in school, using the school environment as an education in being an entrepreneur. In many ways, Steve is getting a different sort of training from being at school than Gregory. What is Steve learning?

Are the young people learning about mixing with each other? Without the experience of seeing the fifth-formers kissing, the chance to watch Dorothy playing football, the chance to meet other people of the opposite sex, surely they would all know far less about how to form relationships. Or would they? Do you think that if Gregory had been to a single-sex school, he would have been able to cope more easily with romance and sexuality?

In the end, of course, all the young people will leave school, as Billy and Gary have done. They will have to make the transition between school and the 'real world'.

When do you think Gregory will leave school? Will he stay on to take his exams, or will he leave now that he is sixteen? Perhaps he will stay on into the sixth form, and take further exams. What do you think?

What will he have gained from being in school? And how does his experience compare to yours? Is your school better, or worse, than Gregory's? Are your teachers more sympathetic, more effective? Has your education, in lessons and out of them, been as good as Gregory's? What would you envy Gregory for, and for what in your education do you think he could envy you?

What do you think are the main messages of the book about education? What is Gerald Cole trying to say about the school system, and about the way the characters like Gregory, Susan, Dorothy and Madeleine are benefiting or suffering from it? In fact, what lessons can we learn from this book, about school, and about education?

SEX AND LOVE

Sex . . . love. What do these words mean to Gregory, and to the other people in the book? They are certainly important; some of the key concepts around which the whole book revolves. So what do they mean, and why are they important?

Let's begin with sex. It seems that for Gregory, as for most of the other boys of his age, it is sexuality that is the focus of interest. They browse through girlie magazines, spy on nurses undressing, dream of having a woman – and often, as in the case of Gary, get one.

Make a list of the boys in the book, and then think about what you know of their attitudes to sex. Some of them have had sexual experience – who? Some of them see sex in terms of tales passed on through magazines. Some of them seem oblivious to sex. Think through these various attitudes that the boys have.

And the adults are not immune. Phil Menzies ogles Miss Welch. The male teachers regard the fifth-form girls as tempting, and not just for their good conversation. Miss Ford sees through Gregory's real reasons for wanting to join the Italian class.

For some, sex can lead to problems. Gregory sees Gary's victory with Fiona as being something to envy (many of the boys are envious of others' sexual prowess), but in fact her pregnancy may very soon lead to difficulties as they are going to marry because they have to. Gregory's ideal of life would be to come home to a woman who would sleep with him – do you think this is a realistic ideal, or is he aiming too high, or too low?

At the start of the book, although an idealist, Gregory seems to focus all his attention on women's physical appearance. They are a wonderful mystery to him, and he doesn't seem to consider that they might have personalities, fears and emotions like he does, that they could be anything but totally confident, sexual beings.

Is this true? What do the girls in the book feel about sexuality? How are the girls' attitudes to sex different? How do they talk about sexuality, how do they approach it? Are they more, or less, at ease with sex than the boys are? Do they want to leap into bed with anyone, as some of the boys think? Is any girl who wants to kiss willing to go further?

What about love? When Gregory meets Dorothy, the one great

love of his life, football seems to blend with his feelings of sexuality to create another great love – that for Dorothy. His whole world changes. He sees things in a totally different way, feels quite different, experiences bursts of emotion – fear, panic, hope, passion. He becomes obsessed with Dorothy, her looks, her words, her skill at football.

There is sexuality here. Gregory certainly fancies Dorothy, though his thoughts are more worshipful than lustful. He describes them as love. He feels that he loves her, and that because of that, she cannot, will not, reject him. Is he right? Do you think Gregory is in love with Dorothy? There are many uses of the word 'love', and it can mean many different things. So think carefully what Gregory means by the word, and then write about whether you think he does love Dorothy or not.

For many of the boys, in fact, there is confusion about what a relationship with a girl involves. Gary has dived headfirst into a sexual relationship, and landed himself with marriage. Steve thinks he will have a relationship with something 'expensive' (p. 50). Andy considers that talking about slaughtered calves will interest women (pp. 98–9).

So what should a relationship between two people involve? Jot down some of your own ideas, and then compare them with the ideas of people in the book. Are they the same, or different?

If you had to give advice to any of the following characters on how to find, and develop, a good relationship, what would you say:

Eric
Andy
Phil Menzies

How would they need to be different, or act differently, in order to get the relationship that they wanted and got something from?

For the girls, things are not the same. They certainly seem to have clearer thoughts, both about what they want and about how to get it.

What do you think Dorothy looks for in a relationship? She responds to Gordon; what do you think motivates her in that relationship? Gregory hears that Dorothy 'knows' someone at the 'physical ed. college' (p. 114); what is she looking for from him? She clearly doesn't love Gregory. She merely tolerates him, and is willing and eager to pass him on to Susan. Do you think Dorothy loves anyone, yet?

What about Madeleine? She gives Gregory advice, and seems totally at ease with, and in control of, her relationship with Richard. Although very young, she is able to brush off the attentions of Billy and tell Richard exactly what she wants. And she acts on her own advice of '*do* it' (p. 83).

What about Susan? She sees Gregory and likes him. She goes about getting him in a subtle and effective way. Read over the scene where Gregory realizes that it is Susan who wants to go out with him, and she offers him the time to think it over (pp. 118–22).

What sort of relationship do you think Susan wants with Gregory? How does she go about helping the relationship to develop? What differences do you notice in the way Susan approaches the problem of their getting on together, as compared with how Gregory has handled Dorothy? Notice the attitudes Susan has which help Gregory to relax, and start to be himself, which enable him really to contact the affection he can begin to feel for her.

Gregory has to change his ideas of love, and he succeeds in doing this. He realizes both that he is not in love with Dorothy, and that being with a girl like Susan is a very different thing. How does his attitude to sex and to love change after he has been with Susan? Do you think these changes are good for Gregory?

What do you think this book is trying to say about sexuality and about love? Which of the following comments do you agree with and which do you disagree with? Give your reasons.

The book is trying to say that sexuality is the most important thing in life.

The book shows that to a young person sexuality is very important.

The book seems to say that young people don't know what love means.

The book tells us that it's natural to feel confused about sexuality.

It's clear from the book that young people fall in love very easily.

The book demonstrates that young love is important in life.

From what happens in the book, you would think that boys don't know how to handle relationships and girls do.

The book strongly condemns young people's attitudes to sex.

Finally, think about the points that the book does make about sex and love. Which of them do you think are right? Does the author give an accurate picture of how young people think about sex and love? Does what he writes ring true for you?

GROWING UP

Gregory's Girl is about growing up. The book begins by telling us that Gregory has grown five inches in the last year; and these changes in physical state are matched by changes in mental and emotional state. Gregory, and all the other young people in the story, are changing. And how they are changing, and the effects of this on their lives, are themes that runs throughout the book.

What do we mean by 'growing up'? The physical changes are obvious. Gregory, along with all his male counterparts, is suffering from the effects of 'hormones', as his father puts it (p. 5). Beards grow, though not as much as their owners want them to. Voices squeak at the most inappropriate moments. Complexions blush and flush when embarrassed. And the boys grow, shooting up to the ceiling in the way just described.

The boys seem to find it all very embarrassing. Their minds struggle with what their bodies are doing. Spots erupt, shaving scars show, sweat pours. Find two or three incidents when the sheer physical effects of becoming adult, the changes of puberty, affect Gregory or his friends. Read the incidents through and compare them with your own, or with your friends', experiences of similar difficulties. What do the boys affected feel and think about what is happening to them?

In contrast, the girls and women in the book seem to have no trouble at all with their physical growth. No spots are mentioned, no trouble with developing breasts or difficult times of the month. As Gordon-John Sinclair remarked, the girls seem to be 'in control'. Is this realistic? Again, compare the way female puberty is presented in the book with any similar experiences you or your friends may have had. What problems can girls have? Why do you think such problems aren't dealt with in the book?

Gregory's emotions, and their strength and changeability, are stressed from the very first words of the book: 'Gregory Underwood was happy.' So the book starts – and ends. In between, Gregory moves through a whole range of feelings, sometimes ecstatic, sometimes painful. Make a list of at least a dozen of the emotions Gregory experiences through the novel. How many of them are strong emotions, how many of them change suddenly? Is this how you have felt while growing up?

Look at other people in the book, boys and girls, young people and older people. How do they feel? Can you spot any 'patterns of feeling' that are the same? Do all the boys feel the same kinds of emotion? Do all the girls appear to feel the same? How far do you agree with the following statements about how feelings are handled by the characters in the book?

All the boys without exception find difficulty in handling their emotions.
All the girls seem to have their emotions under control.
Younger people than Gregory seem to be more self-confident than he is.
All the adults in the book are effective and never uncertain.
Some of the teachers still feel unsure of themselves.
The boys who have left school seem more confident.
The girls seem to feel strong emotions.

One of the effects of growing up seems to be that some things that were important to Gregory suddenly hold no emotional charge for him at all – like football. His whole value system seems to be turning upside-down. What was vital becomes mediocre, and some things that he never noticed before – like girls – become vital.

One of the key issues in growing up is coming to terms with changing feelings of sexuality. Gregory begins the book by being very unsure of what he feels. He knows that the female body turns him on, but he has no experience of sex. He fantasizes, worships from afar, but is unsure of how to go about getting a woman.

It seems as if the same is true for many of his friends. Eric, Andy, Pete and Charlie join him in spying at the nurses' home. Andy in particular spends the whole book trying desperately to get a woman.

He makes mistake after mistake, and in the end has not succeeded. Growing up is about learning skills as well as getting new perspectives on things. What other problems and worries do other boys in the book have?

But some of the boys, and many of the girls, whether by intuition or experience, do seem to know what to do. Steve is very offhand about it all, and we sense that he will succeed with women. Gordon's chat-up technique succeeds with Dorothy. And all the girls seem totally at ease with things sexual, taking the lead in initiating relationships, and eagerly and confidently getting as much sexual experience as they want. In your experience, is this a reflection of what happens in real life?

These three areas then – physical, emotional and sexual – seem to be the three areas that cause most disruption when young people move from being children to being adults. The message of the book is that boys have more trouble in these areas than girls – although you may, as we suggested, want to question this.

But the book goes further in suggesting that these areas can be a problem even when people are out of their teens, that even adults can have a lot of growing up to do. Look at Phil Menzies. He has problems with his moustache, which doesn't seem to grow. He often seems unconfident and unsure, particularly when faced with Gregory. He worries about his sex life, just as the boys do. Do you think Phil Menzies has 'grown up' yet?

Conversely, the two youngest people in the book, Madeleine and Richard, seem to be the most mature. Madeleine is sensible, aware and totally self-confident. She knows, and laughs at, sexual innuendos. She supports Gregory when he takes a girlfriend, and gives him advice on how to cope with his emotions. Richard realizes that Gregory is having problems, and takes an almost fatherly attitude to him.

So, who are the grown-ups? What do we actually mean by 'growing up'? Is it physical change, such as puberty? If so, then Richard and Madeleine are not grown up. Is it emotional change, which leads to a mature understanding of things? If so, then maybe Phil Menzies is not grown up. Or is it a balanced view of sex, love, romance – relationships with the opposite sex? If so, who in the book has grown up?

Certainly, Gregory matures during the course of the book. His physical changes are less noticeable, but emotionally he develops a lot and, particularly in his attitude to women, things change for him.

At first, he falls for Dorothy and goes through agonies of not knowing what to do before he acts. Then, rejected, he grows through that to accept that getting on with Susan, and being accepted by her, is a better basis for a relationship. He begins to forget the nurses' home and the bus driver in favour of a real friendship rather than a fantasy.

Make a full list of the things about Gregory that change during the course of the book, ways in which he 'grows up'. Then write about how he does so.

Who else in the book grows up, if anyone? Lots of people stay as they are. Andy seems stuck in his ineffectuality; Eric still prefers photographs to the real person. Does anyone else grow, change, develop during the course of the book?

The picture of 'growing up' presented in the book is a very particular one. It misses out many things that are important to young people, and many experiences that young people need to have in order to become adult. It doesn't express, for example, the sentiments that Gordon-John Sinclair expressed in his interview, that adolescence 'doesn't last for ever'. It may not reflect your experience of maturing, but do you think that it is a useful comment on what it is like to be a teenager, to be changing, physically, emotionally, sexually? If so, what is useful about it? If not, what could be added to improve it?

BOYS AND GIRLS

One of the main themes in the book is that of gender differences, the differences between boys and girls.

First, make a list of all the characters you can remember, dividing them into male and female. Which group is biggest? Is this the group the book most concentrates on? And which point of view do you think the book is written from, male or female?

Next, go through the list of characters, making notes on their attitudes towards the opposite sex. Do they like them or hate them? Maybe it's a little more complicated than that. Some characters are scared of their opposites, but want to get close to them.

Fill in below the missing details about some of the key characters in the book, explaining their views about the opposite sex and in particular certain members of it:

Gregory feels about girls in general . . .
    about Madeleine
    about Dorothy
    about Susan
    about the nurse
    about the bus driver
Phil Menzies feels about girls in general . . .
    about girls playing football
    about Dorothy
    about Miss Welch
Dorothy feels about men in general . . .
    boys in general
    about Phil Menzies
    about Gregory
Madeleine feels about boys in general . . .
    about Gregory
    about Richard
Andy feels about girls in general . . .
    about Dorothy (at first)
    about Dorothy (in the end)
Steve feels about girls in general . . .

You should by now have a fairly comprehensive idea of the sort of attitudes people in the book have. They are mixed, of course. Gregory feels in turns frightened, attracted, repelled, shunned, comforted and aroused by women. But, in general, he finds them amazing.

What general attitudes do you have about members of the opposite sex? Do you have a picture of what 'girls', 'boys', 'men' or 'women' are like? When you come to think about a particular girl or boy, do you somehow find that they are not as you imagined?

This certainly happens a lot in the book. Dorothy in particular challenges everyone's ideas of what a girl is. She also challenges their idea of what a girl should do, by playing football. As Gordon-John Sinclair said in his interview, 'a girl who can play football . . . what more can you want?' It's interesting, too, that no one seems to notice that Steve, a boy, is expert at cooking, while many people are aghast that a girl is good at football.

Who in the book has 'stereotyped' ideas about the opposite sex? Is it only the older people, or only the younger people? Who seems to be open-minded about what girls, or boys, should do? Are there any people in the book who don't seem to believe in 'equal opportunities', at least at first?

As well as biased attitudes about what boys or girls should do, there are many examples in the book of prejudice or ignorance about what boys and girls do – particularly about sex. Gregory's view of women, when the book opens, is very much based on what he has read, what he has seen through uncurtained windows. Other 'myths' get passed around – look at what Andy believes about women. Very few of the boys see women as other than sexual stereotypes; even Steve puts his hand on Susan's bottom.

But when some people in the book get to know others, then they discover that they are not like their stereotypes at all. Women aren't frightening creatures, eager to take and then devour a man – nor are they desperate for a man, any man. Read over, for example, chapter 12, when Gregory goes out on his first date. He finds Susan easy to get on with, he is not at all overawed. He has fun, and discovers that a girl is a person just like he is, except possibly more mature.

In fact, when we come to look at how the sexes behave, the book seems clearly to favour the girls. Women teachers are self-confident, and they can see right through the boys' feeble excuses. The girls also seem to be self-confident and self-aware. And it is the girls who 'help each other out' (p. 119), who support each other in groups; who are, as Gordon-John Sinclair commented, 'in control'.

Most of all, it is girls like Dorothy and Susan who seem to take action, who initiate, go for what they want. Girls are like Madeleine who is emotionally mature at ten, or like Margo and Carol who lead Gregory gently to where they want him to go.

Choose either Dorothy, Madeleine or Susan and read through the sections of the book where they appear. What impression do we get of them as women? Are they good 'role models' for other women to copy? Are they women that other women could be proud of?

In comparison, the boys seem feeble, wrapped up in their own fear and longing for sexual experience. They hang back, take photos, worry – while the girls are deciding what they want.

Some are strong – Steve knows what he wants, he gets it, he sees the world clearly. Are there any other boys or men in the book who seem to you to be truly self-confident and mature?

Make a list of differences in the book between how boys cope with things and how girls cope with things. Notice ways in which the boys succeed, but also be aware that, in most situations, the girls are in control.

In many ways, the book is written from the boys' point of view, to explore all the horrors of being a boy growing up, of feeling strong emotions and not knowing what to do, of wanting to approach someone and being afraid of rejection. In comparison, to the boys the girls seem like goddesses, totally sure of themselves and able to do what they want.

Is this true? Do you, as a boy or a girl, think that girls always know what to do, are always in command of a situation? Think back in your experience, and those of your friends and people you know. Can you think of examples where girls have been shy or unsure, and have needed encouragement? Are there any examples in the book where this happens?

Would you have preferred the book to have shown more examples of girls feeling as unsure as Gregory does? Would the book have been more effective if it had? Or does the way the book presents the differences between the sexes strike just the right note for you, in presenting women as strong, mature people and men as vulnerable?

HUMOUR

Perhaps one of the most difficult things to write about in the world is humour. For making someone else laugh, or even smile, without meeting them, or seeing whether they are reacting, is very hard.

You might think that *Gregory's Girl* had a head start because it was based on a film, where jokes had already been tried and tested. But remember that translating them into words that work as well as the film is also a difficult task – and always be aware that the book is *not* the film. What works on the screen needs a very particular and skilled choice of words to make it funny on a page, with no pictures and no sound to add to the impact.

There seem to be several sorts of humour in the book. The first sort is simple slapstick, where physical misfortune makes us laugh in sympathy, or in derision. We imagine we are the person in difficulties and laugh in embarrassment, or maybe in fear, that it might happen to us.

What examples of this sort of humour can you find in *Gregory's Girl*? Look particularly at the football matches, or the occasion when Gregory is helping Dorothy practise her goal-scoring. These are times when something quite physically unfortunate is happening to someone, and we are meant to find it funny.

Choose two incidents, preferably ones that make you laugh (though this kind of humour may not always appeal) and read them through. Be careful not to confuse the incident in the book with the incident in the film; there may be differences. For each one, answer these questions:

What happens in the incident?
Who is involved?
What happens that is particularly funny?
Who has the physical misfortune, or suffers?
What pictures do you get in your mind that make the incident seem funny?
How do the words help to make the incident humorous?
What could the writer have done to have described the incident in a funnier way?
Which are the essential bits in each incident that make it funny (in other words which bits would you need to leave out in order to make the incident serious)?

A second form of humour in the book is when people make jokes about or tease other people. Dorothy and the girls laugh at Gregory and his friends in this way. Even Miss Ford teases Gregory. And Gregory's dad teases him when they meet in the car.

This is one person talking about another in a way that is meant to mock. Sometimes this is harmless, as when Mr Underwood is talking to Gregory. But sometimes it is meant to hurt, so it is not quite so humorous. Who in the book does poke fun in a way that is meant to hurt? Who insults other people, or makes comments about them, so that others will laugh?

Choose two of these incidents, again reading them from the book rather than just remembering them from the film. It may be one that makes you smile rather than laugh, or may even make you feel sorry for the person who is at the other end of the joke. Then look again at the questions listed on page 79. Make notes on these new incidents. In particular, ask how funny you really find what is said and done. Do you find it as funny as the people in the book do, or do you see the other, less humorous, side of what is happening?

Another sort of humour, the main sort in the book, is where the person in a scene is unaware that what he or she is doing is actually very humorous. It is what they do naturally, or say naturally, but we laugh at their action for a number of reasons; because it doesn't get the effect they want, because they will later think it silly, because we once behaved like that and don't any more.

In particular, in *Gregory's Girl* many of the things that the boys do are ineffectual because they have no experience. Gregory often tries to do something but it turns out badly or he looks a fool. And one of the reasons we can laugh is because we remember feeling like that ourselves, a long time ago or recently, and know that we probably looked silly too.

This is not cruel laughter. We don't laugh at Gregory because he misunderstands the lady bus driver, or at Andy because he is unintentionally nauseating Margo and Carol, or at Phil Menzies because he is scared of Gregory. We laugh with them because part of us identifies with them and feels sorry for them – and we have to laugh.

Again, choose two incidents, particularly ones which you can identify with. You might choose ones that have happened to you, or ones which you have seen happen to your friends – ones which ring a bell of recognition, a sigh of 'Oh, I did that.'

Ask the questions on p. 79 about each of these incidents. Then ask particularly what it is about the incident that you recognize, what makes you identify with the person involved, what makes you laugh in sympathy.

There are other kinds of humour in the book. You might like to track down some of them for yourself, and find out what it is about them particularly that makes you laugh or smile, groan or roll about laughing.

Do you feel that *Gregory's Girl* is a humorous book? If you were writing it, would you have added any incidents and, if so, what would they have been? Would you have left any of the humorous incidents out, because they simply don't work, or because you feel they don't add to what the book is trying to say?

All the humour is meant to make a point. As we laugh, we are supposed to be realizing something. In the case of slapstick, perhaps we are meant to be realizing how painful it is physically to cope with growing up, having to struggle to get someone's admiration at lunch-time on the football pitch. In the case of jokes and teasing, perhaps we are meant to realize how cruel people can be about others. And in the case of humour based on someone only becoming aware later what they have done, maybe we are meant to realize that growing up involves doing things that, later, we regret; and that, later, are totally unimportant.

Mostly, the humour in *Gregory's Girl* is kind humour, meant to make us sympathize with the characters, not mock them cruelly. It is a humour that adds to our liking for them, and does not make us despise them.

Passages for Comparison

Friendship Poems

1

There's good mates and bad mates
  'Sorry to keep you waiting' mates
Cheap skates and wet mates
  The ones you end up hating mates
Hard mates and fighting mates
  Witty and exciting mates
Mates you want to hug
  And mates you want to clout
Ones that get you into trouble
  And ones that get you out.

2

Two's company
One's lonely.

3

I'm a fish out of water
I'm two left feet
On my own and lonely
I'm incomplete

I'm boots without laces
I'm jeans without a zip
I'm lost, I'm a zombie
I'm a dislocated hip.

4

When you're young
Love sometimes confuses
It clouds the brain
And blows the fuses
How often during those tender years
You just can't see the wood for the tears.

From *Sky in the Pie*, Roger McGough

Getting Off the Mark

The polling station was a local school. Straggling past the school, as I went in, were two pairs of teenage girls and two pairs of teenage boys.

Each pair independent of the others. Walking, according to sex, in opposite directions.

Coming out of the school, I was surprised to see the same two pairs of teenage girls and the same two pairs of teenage boys.

Still walking in opposite directions. But this time, if you follow me, in OPPOSITE opposite directions.

Clearly, they'd all been to their respective ends of the street, then retraced their steps. But why? They weren't taking a constitutional, because teenagers don't take constitutionals. They weren't waiting for their mums, because they would have regarded themselves as above the mum-waiting age. They weren't demonstrating for votes at fifteen, because they didn't have placards. So what were they up to?

Then, as the first pair of girls passed the second pair of boys, I saw two sets of female shoulders shaking in a repressed fit of the giggles. And the penny dropped. What I'd stumbled across was the local duck-walk.

If you do not know what a duck-walk is, have no fear. I am about to tell you more about the subject than you can possibly need to know.

A duck-walk is a length of pavement, stretch of recreation ground, boating-lake perimeter, park-bandstand circumference, shopping-parade diameter, or any other form of measured mile give or take a hundred yards or so, where the lads and lasses of the town perambulate in the hope of – to use the phrase of my own long-lost youth – getting off with each other.

The British in Love
by Jilly Cooper, Aslington Books, London, 1980

Valentine Poem

> If I were a poet
> I'd write poems for you.
> If I were a musician,
> Music too.
> But as I'm only an average man
> I give you my love
> As best what I can.
>
> If I were a sculptor
> I'd sculpt you in stone.
> An osteopath,
> Work myself to the bone.
> But as I'm just a man in the street
> I give you my love,
> Lay my heart at your feet
>
> > > > (*ugh!*)
>
> If I were an orator
> I'd make pretty speeches.
> An oil tanker,
> Break up on your beaches.
> But as I'm just an ordinary Joe
> I send you my love,
> As best what I know.

From *Sky in the Pie*, Roger McGough

Glossary

abated: lessened.
abject: grovelling, humbled.
adamantine: definite.
adjacent: next to.
affably: in a friendly way.
affirmative: positive.
altercation: argument.
altruism: kindness.
ambled: walked slowly.
animatedly: in a lively way.
anticipated: expected.
anticipation: looking forward to.
antipathy: intense dislike.
apocalypse: end of the world.
appalled: horrified.
arpeggios: musical term for a running
   succession of notes.
atypically: not typical.
aura: atmosphere: surrounding air.

banter: teasing language.
basking: sunning herself.
beacon: light.
befuddled: confused.
belligerent: aggressive.
bemused: confused.
benediction: blessing.
benign: kind.
benignity: kindness.
berserkers: Ancient Norse warriors who
   worked themselves up into an insane
   frenzy before going into battle.
bizarre: strange.
blanch: pale.
bland: mild.
blasé: unconcerned.
blatant: open.

blatantly: obviously.
bonhomie: good-nature: friendliness.

caressed: stroked gently.
caterwauling: yowling.
catholic: varied.
chagrin: annoyance.
chastisement: punishment: telling-off.
chided: scolded.
clique: small, exclusive group.
cogitation: thought.
concede: give in.
conciliatory: making amends.
concurred: agreed.
confrontation: face-to-face fight.
consternation: amazement.
corroborate: confirm.
cosmic: of the universe.
covertly: secretly.
coyly: shyly.
craved: wanted very much.
credentials: proof of identity.
cuisine: cooking.

decisive: definite.
decrying: mocking.
deflected: knocked aside.
dejectedly: sadly.
delirium: raving.
depravities: sexual misdoings.
deprecatingly: in a belittling way.
derisive: mocking.
designated: worked out: intended.
deviousness: cleverly underhand.
diffuse: dispersed.
diminutive: tiny.

dire: dreadful.

discernible: noticeable.

disconcerted: confused: made uncertain.

disconcerting: unbalancing.

disconsolately: dejectedly.

discreet: tactfully reserved: to keep private.

disdain: despise.

dishevelled: untidy.

disparate: separate.

dourly: solemnly.

druidic: priestly: hypnotic.

duffers: dull or incompetent persons.

effusive: over-talkative.

effusively: exuberantly: extravagantly.

elated: excited.

elucidation: explanation.

elude: miss: escape.

embezzler: person who dishonestly diverts others' money into his own pocket.

emboldened: made bold.

emitted: gave out.

emphatically: firmly.

enclave: protected territory.

ennumerator: counter.

entrepreneur: a person who runs a business for profit.

equanimity: a balanced viewpoint.

euphoria: extreme happiness.

exhorting: encouraging.

exorcised: removed completely.

explicit: open.

exulting: glorying, enjoying immensely.

fastidiously: with great care.

ferocity: fierceness.

flippant: light-hearted.

flummoxed: confused.

foist: palm off.

foliage: leaves.

forte: strong point.

furtively: secretively.

gaggle: chattering group.

galumphing: leaping clumsily.

gawky: ungainly.

Genghis Khan: Mongol conqueror in the 12th century A.D.

glibly: smoothly.

gluteus maximus: medical term for a person's backside or bottom.

gothic: medieval (style of writing).

gouged: dug out.

groundswell: undercurrent of opinion.

hamlet: small village.

harpies: vicious women of mythology.

heady: inebriating.

hiatus: pause.

horde: crowd.

icummen: old English expression, 'coming'.

imminence: nearness.

immune: untouched.

impetus: drive.

imploringly: asking earnestly.

impotently: powerlessly.

inadvertently: unintentionally, by accident.

inanely: foolishly.

incipient: at the early stage of development.

incredulous: amazed.

indisputably: undoubtedly.

inebriated: drunk.

ineptitude: inefficiency.

inexorably: relentlessly.

infatuation: foolish or extravagant passion.

infiltrate: get into and mix with.

infuriate: annoy.

infuriated: very annoyed.

inordinately: extremely.

insensate: unfeeling.

insidiously: slyly: with cunning.

interrogatively: questioningly.

intimacy: closeness.

inured: used to.

jaded: overworked.
jubilant: happy: triumphant.

kaput: literally from German, meaning 'broken' or 'ruined'.

largesse: abundance.
lasciviously: lustfully.
latent: hidden.
leaden: heavy.
leered: glanced evilly.
levity: lightness.
lithe: athletic.
loped: walked with long strides.
lothario: a rake: one who seduces.
lugubriously: dismally.
lunacy: madness.
lurid: distasteful.

machinations: intrigues.
magnanimous: gracious.
malevolent: evil.
malicious: vicious.
malignant: evil.
maniac: mad person.
manifested: made evident.
marginally: slightly.
melancholia: sadness.
melancholic: sad.
melee: crowd.
mellowing: softening (growing dark).
mesmeric: hypnotic.
mollified: soothed.
monotone: one tone of voice.
mute: silent.

naivety: innocence.
nape: back of the neck.
niche: place.
non-committal: undecided.
non-sequiturs: remarks that don't follow.
nonchalance: lack of concern.

nonchalantly: casually.
notoriously: infamously.

obliquely: at an angle.
oblivious: unaware of.
obnoxious: awful.
obtuse: emotionally insensitive.
olive branch: peace offering.
onslaught: attack.
operative: worker.
ostentatious: showy.
ostentatiously: showing off.

pampering: excessively comfortable.
paranoid: insanely fearful.
parody: feeble imitation.
parrying: quick defensive moves.
peeved: resentful: annoyed.
pensively: thoughtfully.
perplexed: confused.
phalanx: battle line.
phantom: imaginary.
pirouetted: spun round.
placated: pleased, calmed.
ploy: tactic.
pompous: proud.
precocious: early developer.
predicament: problem.
premonition: warning: sense of danger.
prevailing: most common.
proprietorally: like an owner.
pubescent: adolescent.
pugnacious: aggressive.
pummelling: punching.
purgatory: place of suffering.

quibbling: making trivial objections.
quirky: humorously odd.
quixotic: idealistic.
quizzical: questioning.

rabid: mad.
rakish: dissipated.
rampant: wild.
randy: sexually excitable.

rank disbelief: total reluctance to believe.
rapine: seizure by force.
rapt: fascinated: concentrated.
rasped: scraped: scratched.
raucous: loud and vulgar.
recriminations: blame.
recumbent: lying down.
redeeming: saving.
redressed: put right.
regime: rule.
rejuvenated: made younger.
remnants: remainder.
reprimand: telling off.
reproof: expression of criticism.
resolute: determined.
resolution: determination.
reverie: dream.
rigor mortis: stiffness of death.
roseate: rosy.

sagely: wisely.
sallies: excursions.
sardonic: mocking.
scathing: criticize strongly.
scram: go.
scrutiny: close examination.
seething: angry.
seraphically: angelically.
serene: calm and happy.
skittered: ran lightly.
smirk: satisfied grin.
smug: contented.
sordid: dirty.
spastic: unco-ordinated.
speakeasy: illegal liquor shop.
speculative: wondering.
stalwartly: bravely.
stemmed: stopped.
suave: sophisticated.
subterfuge: plot.
subtlety: disguised meaning.

suffused: flushed.
sward: grass.
sycophantic: flattering: toadying.

tardiness: lateness.
taut: tightly stretched.
telepathy: communication by thought.
tentative: hesitant.
tousle-haired: dishevelled.
toying: playing.
trek: journey.
tremulous: trembling.
trepidation: fear.

unabashed: unashamed.
unfeigned: unpretended.
unkempt: untidy.
unperturbed: unworried.
unsimulated: real.
unsullied: unspoiled.
urbanely: with sophistication.
usurpation: take-over.

vacated: left empty.
vaulted: leapt.
vexation: irritation.
vindictive: revengeful.
visage: face.
voluble: talkative.

waned: lessened.
wanly: palely.
waxed eloquent: spoke with enthusiasm.
weal: good.
will o'wisp: pale, flickering light.
wreak: to inflict.
wry: dryly humorous.

zabaglione: Italian pudding made with
   whipped eggs and sugar.
zaniness: madness.

Examination Questions

Before tackling the examination questions given below, you may find it helpful to think about the following very general questions about *Gregory's Girl*.

1. Do you think the plot of *Gregory's Girl* is realistic? Have any of the things that happened to Gregory and Dorothy ever happened to you?
2. Do you know anyone like Gregory? Do you sympathize with his problems?
3. Do you think Gregory's comprehensive school gives the pupils a good education? How could it improve?
4. What are your experiences of growing up? Do they make you feel anything like Gregory did? Do you think boys and girls react differently to adolescence?
5. Is *Gregory's Girl* funny? Why? Why not?
6. What did you think of the film of *Gregory's Girl*? Would you recommend it to anyone else? Would you recommend reading the book to someone who has seen the film?

THE GCSE EXAMINATION

In this examination you may find that the set texts have been selected by your teacher from a very wide list of suggestions in the examination syllabus. The questions in the examination paper will therefore be applicable to many different books. Here are some questions that you could answer by making use of *Gregory's Girl*.

1. Choose any book you have read which deals with school life. Show how the author describes the school, its staff and the pupils, and whether you think that the description is effective.
2. Write about any book you have studied in which the author examines love. Choose two characters in this book and show how their views to love differ.
3. Consider any book you have read which has also been produced as a film or television film. Consider carefully which version you prefer, and say why. There is no need to tell the story.
4. Choose any book you know that is about people of your own age. Consider how successfully an author who is older than you has portrayed what it is like to be someone young.
5. Choose an incident from a book you have read which involves someone feeling a strong emotion. Say how the author uses the incident to show the emotion felt, and mention some of the ways in which he or she does it.
6. Humour can help us to understand serious issues. With reference to a book you have studied, show how this can be done.

QUESTIONS ON *GREGORY'S GIRL*

1. Choose two incidents in *Gregory's Girl* which strongly affect the way the plot is moving. Explain how they do this, and comment on whether you agree with the author's decision to include them.
2. Compare and contrast Dorothy and Susan. Do you think Gregory ended up with the right person?
3. Choose two of the school staff mentioned in the book and comment on their characters. How do they add to the impact of the book?
4. Does Gregory grow up in the course of the book? If so, how? And why?
5. Comment on Madeleine's character in the light of the title of the book.
6. How true is the comment '*Gregory's Girl* is a book about two infatuations – neither of them serious'?